COMPETING
BIBLICALLY

"Tim has offered here the complete and unequivocal handbook to competing biblically! I took so many notes, dog-eared so many pages; it's fun to read a book from someone who coached you and transformed you deeply over the years. I'm going to buy so many copies and give them to all the athletes I know! Thanks, Tim!"

Jefferson Bethke
New York Times Bestselling Author of
Jesus > Religion and *It's Not What You Think*,
Co-Host of *The Real Life Podcast*

"*Competing Biblically* is not only a great book, but what a great title also! The word "competing" shows up usually in the sports world. But what I love about both the title and content of Coach Tim Kuykendall's book is that it is a necessary overflow of biblical centeredness in sports, as it is transferable into Business, Art, Music, Education, Construction, Politics—every talent we perform and every activity we do. When one thinks of the opposition that's directed to the person and work of Christ and His followers today, it is vital for us to learn the principles of—you guessed it—*competing biblically*.

It is very challenging to continually remember that sports or any endeavor is not to become an idol, nor another temptation to worship ourselves. In *Competing Biblically*, Coach Tim takes us through the needed application of using sports to glorify Jesus Christ as its major aim, with biblical directives and applications from God's Word, the Bible.

What's thrilling for me is that when youngsters are coached and parented by biblical teaching in sports, this teaching will last forever. Most of our children won't become pros, but *Competing Biblically* will transfer wonderfully into the competitive world that God directs them to."

Coach Ron Brown
Assistant Football Coach
University of Nebraska
and Co-founder of Kingdom Sports Ministry

"This handbook isn't just theory—it's the playbook Tim and his team practice daily, and reading it is an invitation to join him in a journey of Christ-exalting competition. Whether you are a player, parent, coach, official, or spectator, you will want to learn how to integrate faith and athletics from someone who embodies both—this is the book you need."

Justin Erickson
Author of *7 Friendships Every Man Needs*
Founder of Hardwired Coaching Consulting Firm,
and It Stands Written Ministry

"The words and lessons expressed in this textbook can be trusted because they come from someone fully surrendered to Jesus and who has been in the trenches working out the philosophy as a coach, father, and athletic director. Tim has gleaned wisdom from the saints who have passed the parables of sport and timeless truths down to empower us to preach the gospel, set the captives free, and make disciples in sport. This textbook will transform the reader and everyone they impact in sport. Congratulations, Tim, on blessing the Kingdom of God with a profound tool that has been bathed in prayer to become a weapon to keep the faith and fight the good fight in sport."

Randy Chambers
Founder of 4 Coaches International
Leadership Coach with Coaches of Excellence

"An absolute game-changer! This is the clearest blueprint I've seen for using sports as a tool for Kingdom impact. Tim's wisdom in this book isn't just about sports—it's about forming character, living with purpose, and building God's Kingdom in the arena. Every leader who touches the lives of athletes needs to see this."

Brandon Turner
Host of *TheBetterLife* Podcast
Author of six books, including
The Book on Rental Property Investing, and
How to Invest in Real Estate
Founder and Managing Member of OpenDoor Capital

"Scotty's articulation of the integration of faith and sport changed the trajectory of my life as a college athlete. Tim has put into print many of the principles that confronted the idols of my heart and launched Tim and me into full-time sports ministry. Whether you're an athlete, parent, coach, or spectator, this book will give you practical handles to transform your sports experience FOR the glory of God, and for your ultimate joy and satisfaction through God's great gift of sport."

Brian Peterson
Executive Director and Co-founder of Reality Sports

COMPETING BIBLICALLY

A HANDBOOK

FOR COACHES, ATHLETES, AND PARENTS

Tim Kuykendall
with Scotty Kessler

CROSS TRAINING

Competing Biblically: A Handbook for Coaches, Athletes, and Parents
First Edition Trade Book, 2025
© 2025 by Tim Kuykendall

Unless otherwise indicated, Scriptures are taken from the Holy Bible, New International Version®, NIV®. Copyright © 1973, 1978, 1984, 2011 by Biblica, Inc.™ Used by permission of Zondervan. All rights reserved worldwide. www.zondervan.com The "NIV" and "New International Version" are trademarks registered in the United States Patent and Trademark Office by Biblica, Inc.™

Scriptures marked ES are from the ESV® Bible (The Holy Bible, English Standard Version®), © 2001 by Crossway, a publishing ministry of Good News Publishers. Used by permission. All rights reserved. The ESV text may not be quoted in any publication made available to the public by a Creative Commons license. The ESV may not be translated in whole or in part into any other language."

To order additional books:
www.crosstrainingpublishing.com
www.amazon.com

For questions, bulk discounts on book orders, or to have the author speak at your event, visit:
competingbiblically.com

ISBN: 978-1-929478-88-0

Editorial and Book Packaging: Inspira Literary Solutions, Gig Harbor, Washington

Published by Cross Training Publishing
Omaha, Nebraska

Printed in the USA

We would like to dedicate this book to all the coaches, athletes, and parents that have been in our network of leadership that have made the decision to integrate faith and sport:

- *those who have had the revelation in their hearts that sport can be used as a vehicle to evangelize and disciple for the cause of Christ*
- *those who have decided to use sport to display the Kingdom of God at every practice, workout and contest*
- *those who are giving it their best shot to compete according To the Word of God, By the power of God, For the glory of God.*

We would also like to dedicate this book to the individuals who are hearing, for the first time, the Competing Biblically *philosophy of competition. We pray that you would be inspired to develop a philosophy of competition that has a biblical foundation. We invite you to implement the principles of* Competing Biblically *into your athletic experience, whether as a coach, athlete, parent, or fan.*

TABLE OF CONTENTS

FOREWORD

By Wes Neal

One summer, after I had spoken at a Christian sports camp in Missouri—a high school soccer player came up to me and said, "Wes, being aware of God during my competition doesn't work." The young athlete was referring to what I had taught athletes the previous summer about always being mindful of God's presence.

"How do you mean, it doesn't work?"

"I tried it in our biggest game. There was so much going on that I couldn't think about God being present." Then he shook his head and, again, emphasized, "Too many distractions. It doesn't work."

"Did you try being aware of God's presence during the week of practices leading up to the big game?" I asked.

"No, I wanted to save it just for the game. You know, to give me an edge." We both had a good laugh after I explained that being aware of God's presence was for everyday life, not just for a big game.

"If you would have practiced it during the week, both on and off the field, you would have had it for the big game." Sadly, we Christ-Followers can be just as wrong as the young soccer player. We can wrongly save competing biblically for our "big game," or when we think we might need it.

Truth is, we need competing biblically for all the challenges of everyday life, not just for those in our sports. We seldom know when we will have a "big game" challenge. One can hit us suddenly, without any warning—like a car accident, report of bad news, season-ending injury, unexpected change in plans, sudden turbulent weather, health crisis, betrayal, financial disaster, pang of jealousy, or even someone's careless remark. Here's the thing. If we live biblically in all the arenas of life, we will compete biblically in the sports arena—the big games and the routine practices. Your coaching, parenting, or competing as an athlete is an extension of who you are as a Christ-Follower.

Competing biblically connects us to God, and we need that connection *all the time* in this upside-down world, just as a deep-sea diver needs the connection of an air hose. Without it, he drowns. Without being connected to God, we drown. In fact, you might think of it that way. Competing biblically is to coaches, athletes, or parents, as an air hose is to a deep-sea diver. It connects you to God.

Tim Kuykendall, along with his mentor, coach Scotty Kessler, will help you make that breath-of-life connection through the pages of this book. Here's a suggestion: don't think of this book as simply another book to read. Rather, think of yourself as sitting down with Tim, perhaps in a coffee shop, and "listening" to him enthusiastically pass on to you how competing biblically through the To-By-For approach has impacted his life—including every phase of his coaching.

Scotty will join the two of you every now and then to pass on to you what the legendary Hall of Fame football coach, Frosty Westering, passed on to him. You will benefit from the wisdom Scotty gained from years of experience as he passed the concepts surrounding competing biblically on to Tim. Now, it's Tim's turn to pass this supernatural approach on to you.

In your first coffee shop talk with Tim, you'll smile and then laugh as he tells you about the water bottle-throwing incident. You'll be tuned in as he shares with you many wonderful happenings—as well as embarrassing mishaps—along the way.

In your coffee shop sit-downs with Tim, he will help you grasp for yourself the To-By-For approach in *Competing Biblically.* Hopefully, just as Frosty passed it on to Scotty, just as Scotty passed it on to Tim, and just as Tim passes it on to you, you will pass on the philosophy and practice of competing biblically to those in your own sphere of influence.

And the Kingdom grows. To God be all the glory!

I hope you enjoy "listening" to a very enthusiastic Tim Kuykendall on the pages of this book as much as I did.

Your fellow Christ-Follower,

Wes Neal
Author of *The Handbook on Athletic Perfection: A Training Manual for Christian Athletes*

PREFACE

By Scotty Kessler

My life was completely transformed—spiritually, mentally, emotionally, and physically—while playing, coaching, and living under the leadership of Frosty Westering at Pacific Lutheran University in Tacoma, Washington. The quantity of impact from Frosty and the PLU Football family upon my life's story is more than I could have ever imagined. Bottom line—I am who I am because of my relationships within the PLU football community that Frosty stewarded. Ultimately, Frosty was a divine gift to Pacific Lutheran University specifically, and to the world of sport in general, and I mean divine in every sense of the word.

In addition, the PLU Football and the EMAL (Every Man A Lute) philosophy of competition (which Frosty called "More than Winning") is the single most eternally impactful sport-related philosophy, and more importantly philosophy of life, that I have ever read about, heard of, seen, or experienced—ever! Nothing is even close. The direct impact of this philosophy on the lives of men and women, boys and girls, and the subsequent extended ripple effect upon parents, families, and others is incalculable. It changed my entire life trajectory and planted the seeds for what would become what I call "competing biblically," rooted in the teachings and practice of Frosty Westering and Wes Neal.

Tim and I are very excited for this book to be published. We have spent many hours over the last 17 years discussing *Competing Biblically* as a philosophy of competition integrating sport and faith. Part of that collaboration has been through our association with Kingdom Sports, a ministry co-founded by our friends and brothers-in-Christ, Gordon Thiessen and Ron Brown. Kingdom Sports was founded to instruct future generations of coaches and athletes on how to compete biblically and has in many ways served as a melting pot for the knowledge, insight, and experience we have gained through our own faith walks and through friends and mentors such as Frosty and Wes.

Tim and I have desired for many years to put something into print that could be an ongoing resource for those who wish to learn about the concepts and practice of the Competing Biblically Philosophy. It is through Cross Training Publishing, the publishing arm for Kingdom Sports, and its Bible study guides and books on competing biblically, that we were able to make this book a reality. I pray that this book will serve as a catalyst for you to understand what the Lord Jesus has taught us through God's Word regarding how to compete biblically.

Additionally, Tim and I are on the same page in every way regarding the following manuscript. Though Tim did all the writing, we are in full agreement with what and how things were articulated within the text. Consequently, whoever of us appears to be "speaking" at any given point, please consider that it is one voice with the hope and belief that the Holy Spirit has led and guided us through this process and project.

Scotty Kessler

INTRODUCTION

By Tim Kuykendall

There are many philosophies of competition proposed by legitimate and sincere professing believers regarding competition. These philosophies emphasize various approaches to sport—mentally, emotionally, physically, and spiritually.

Scotty Kessler and I consider *Competing Biblically* as our distinct philosophy—a way to think about competition, though not THE only way. This philosophy originates largely from two key figures: Wes Neal (who kindly wrote the Foreword for this book) and Frosty Westering, both of whom we will discuss in Chapter 2 and throughout the book. The core principles of our approach are rooted in their philosophies on competition.

Various organizations across the country emphasize a philosophy of competition within Christian ministry, each with its own flavor. For example, some refer to it as "More Than Winning," a term associated with Frosty Westering. Others use terms like "More Than Champions," or "Make the Big Time Where You Are." Wes Neal termed it "Total Release Performance," while an organization in Washington State, called Reality Sports, of which I am a co-founder, refers to it as "Competing Upside Down."

These philosophies may be articulated differently based on personalities, cultural contexts, and frames of reference, but they share similar threads and core beliefs. We intend to share these perspectives and insights based on our understanding and experience. We believe sport is one of the very few and powerful international languages, meaning every country in the world has some kind of sport context. Music is another example. If these are universal languages, we believe it is worthwhile to have a conviction about a biblical philosophy of competition.

It is important to have a conviction and be humble about it. If you have a conviction but do not have humility, that can come across as arrogance. If you have humility without conviction, you may lack direction. A balance of conviction and humility is necessary for effective leadership and innovation.

The phrase "competing biblically" was developed for our way of thinking. There are two groups of people in the world, the lost and the saved. The lost need evangelism and the saved need to grow as learners and followers of Jesus Christ. This involves both evangelism and discipleship. We use sport not only as an outreach tool but also within communities for discipleship. So, this book is not only about sport; it is about using sport to develop a comprehensive philosophy of life, not just a philosophy of competition.

The principles and concepts of this approach are transferable to many aspects of living. This represents a holistic lifestyle, integrated into everything we do. The transferability of the principles, concepts, and truths of *Competing Biblically* can be applied to everyday living. We view this as a lifestyle, specifically a Great Commission lifestyle undergirded by a biblical philosophy of competition. These elements are integrated in our approach, where sport, evangelism, and discipleship are interconnected. We discuss the integration of faith and sport, viewing sport not as an isolated activity but as a fundamental part of life. Individuals are considered sons and daughters of God, whether they are involved in sport through coaching, playing, or spectating.

Statistics in America reflect the significant interaction people have with sport, and individuals will be influenced by the philosophy they adopt and how they integrate their faith with sport. The concept of *Competing Biblically* was developed as a response to the numerous varying philosophies encountered in the realm of sports. We believed that our approach to sports should adhere to biblical principles. As we evaluated our methods of play and coaching through this lens, anything that did not align with biblical teachings was deemed unacceptable. It was crucial to maintain this firm stance because merging different philosophies could lead to a loss of distinctiveness. Our commitment to a biblical philosophy of competition sets us apart from other approaches in both the secular and Christian sports communities.

The distinctiveness of *Competing Biblically* can be observed in three primary areas: our perspective on the scoreboard and the concept of winning and losing, our conduct during play, including interactions with opponents, and our respect towards officials or referees. These aspects differentiate our experience and philosophy from others. And it all tends to show up as we walk about game day; within the game-day setting, our heart opens out: what is our attitude toward winning and losing? What is our attitude toward our opponents and referees?

It's all nice in the classroom setting, but until it goes out into the grass or onto the court, it's only theory. The grass or the court are where the rubber meets the road in terms of where people are. You rub against their flesh and certain terms of their own desires, goals, and agenda. Is it about our will or is it about God's will? Whose will do we want done? What is the process like?

The problem we have found, with many of those who confess His name, is that if they feel good about an outcome, then they deem it "biblical" because they pray after the game, or they acknowledge God after the game. However, their process may be completely UNbiblical when you consider their speech or their behavior *during* the game. That would be unacceptable to us within the spectrum of this philosophy.

The WHAT is competing biblically. The WHY is because we want to make sure we're obedient in every regard, whether it's in sport or in life. The HOW is where the tricky part comes. The HOW has to do with the performance, the process, and that's where it gets difficult. We can have people agree on "The What," and they can agree on "The

Why," but "The How"—the practice—is where the rubber meets the road.

I developed a *Competing Biblically* tree to better grasp this philosophy. The tree's strong root system includes the four pillars and six foundations (we call these "the overs"). At the trunk, prayer is crucial for transferring nutrients to the branches. The branches represent the four blessings, leading to observable outcomes.

Sequence of the Tree:
Roots—4 Pillars (S.U.B.S) and 6 Overs
Trunk—Prayer
Branches—4 Blessings
Fruit—Display of the 9 attitudes of an athlete/fruit of the Spirit

Part	Description
Roots	4 Pillars and 6 Overs
Trunk	Prayer
Branches	4 Blessings
Fruit	Display of the 9 Attitudes of an Athlete/ Fruit of the Spirit

Our target audience encompasses a broad spectrum, not limited to individuals involved in athletics. This philosophy extends beyond sports, impacting businesses, churches, sales groups, and even stay-at-home parents, based on widely acknowledged teachings. It is derived from over 40 years of observing various teaching, coaching, and leadership methods and identifying those that produce long-lasting results. While not the first to explore the integration of faith and sport, this approach has developed a small but growing network nationwide. Scotty Kessler and I developed the Competing Biblically class at Faith International University in Tacoma, Washington, under the Wes Neal School of Sports Ministry. In seeking relevant books, we eventually

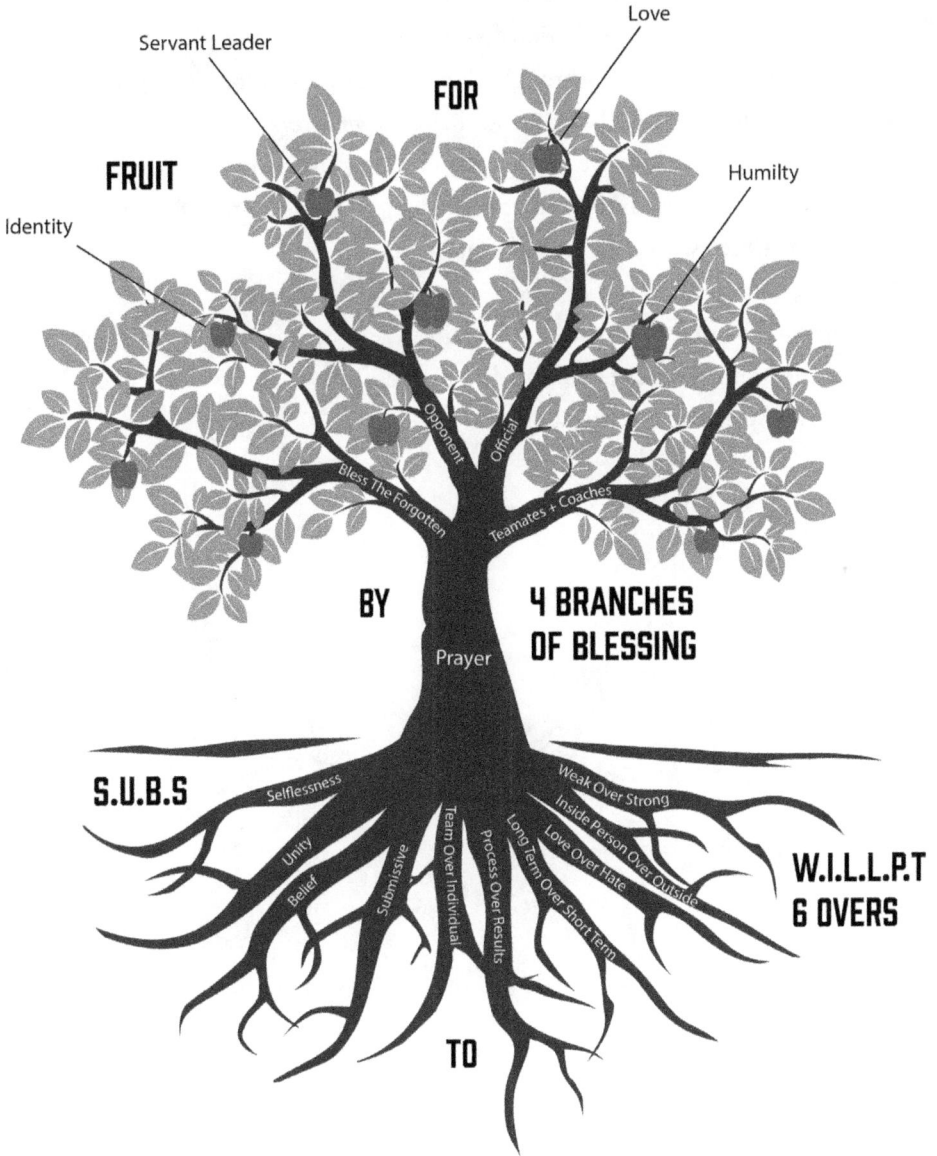

Love

Servant Leader

FOR

FRUIT

Humilty

Identity

Opponent

Official

Bless The Forgotten

Teamates + Coaches

BY

4 BRANCHES
OF BLESSING

Prayer

S.U.B.S

Selflessness

Weak Over Strong

Inside Person Over Outside

Unity

Love Over Hate

W.I.L.L.P.T
6 OVERS

Belief

Submissive

Team Over Individual

Process Over Results

Long Term Over Short Term

TO

compiled our own comprehensive perspective on competition through notebooks, lectures, and various resources.

Now, we have finally brought those writings and resources together to create the book you hold in your hands, *Competing Biblically.* In this book, we explore how we can use the power of the gospel to transform the world of sports and bring about redemption and restoration in the lives of athletes, coaches, and parents alike.

It's time for many of us to start thinking differently about our approach to sports ministry and begin to see the potential for change that lies within each of us. Let's dive in and discover how we can "compete biblically" in the arena of sport.

Tim Kuykendall

SECTION 1

The What and the Why of Competing Biblically

CHAPTER 1

THE POWER OF SPORT

"Sport has the power to change the world."
—Nelson Mandela

*"It (sport) has the power to unite people in a way that little else does.
Sport can awaken hope where there was previously only despair.
Sport speaks to people in a language they understand."*
—Nelson Mandela

The words of Nelson Mandela ring loudly. If you have competed, coached, or participated as a fan in the arena of sport, you are an eyewitness to its power. All around the world, there are millions of fields, arenas, stadiums, and gymnasiums where this power to unite, give hope in the place of despair, and speak to people in a language they understand is literally played out.

As believers in Jesus Christ who have a desire to live out the Great Commission, these are FIELDS that are truly "ripe for the harvest" (see Mt. 9:38, 28:19–20). If we as followers of Jesus have a desire to fulfill the two mandates of the Church to 1) evangelize and 2) disciple, then the arena of Sport is one of the best places to do so. Listen to these staggering statistics of the sheer number of participants in these "fields ripe for harvest" (John 4:25, ESV):

- In America alone, there are 40 million youth participating in organized sports.
- The NFHS (National Federation of High Schools) boasts eight million student athletes.
- According to the International Basketball Federation, there are 610 million people playing basketball worldwide. 220 million in badminton, 60 million playing golf, 265 million in soccer, 300 million playing table tennis/ping pong, and 36.5 million playing pickleball.
- Over 128 countries have national baseball teams affiliated with the World Baseball Softball Confederation (WBSC). Field hockey is played in 100 countries on five continents.
- There are five million soccer refs in the world.
- It is estimated that four billion people watched the last World Cup.
- According to the *World Sports Encyclopedia*, there are 8,000 indigenous sports and sporting games. The world loves sports!

Shaping Worldviews

George Barna, in his latest research and book, *Raising Spiritual Champions*, shows that a person's worldview starts developing in the 15-month-old to 18-month-old range and is largely in place by the age of 13.* That's the prime window of opportunity for discipleship. If a person is not inclined by the time they reach high school to buy into the claims of Christ and the practices He preached, the chances of

---

* Barna, George. *Raising Spiritual Champions: Nurturing Your Child's Heart, Mind and Soul.* Glendale, AZ: Arizona Christian University Press, 2023.

them ever doing so are slim, and the probability gets slimmer with each passing year they are alive.

Strategically, what can we do to make an impact with discipleship before the age of 13? How can coaches and athletes make disciples that make disciples, particularly with younger athletes under the age of 13? Those seven-to-13-year-old kids are coming to a field or gym near you. They are coming by the millions. The biggest youth groups in the nation are not at our churches; they are in our athletic facilities and parks. Should we try to get our kids into church? For sure! However, might we be more effective with a plan of action and discipleship to take to the mission sports field? What can we do with high school and college athletes in both evangelism and discipleship during those crucial times of their lives?

I agree with George Barna and his conclusion that "it is during a person's first dozen years on Earth that they amass the knowledge, relationships, experiences, and wisdom that shape their lifelong perspectives on how the world works, their place in that world, and how they will carry out their vision of self and life for the duration of their stay on the planet."* I would add (how dare I add to George Barna?) that, since many families have their kids involved in sports, the coach and philosophy of *Competing Biblically* is of utmost importance.

The Dynamic Role of Sports in Our Lives

Have you had monumental events or experiences in your past that shaped your entire life? You may not have known it at the time it was happening, but as you look back, you can say with certainty that those times defined who you are today. For me, sports and athletics have provided a multitude of memories and life-changing moments too numerous to count. And out of all the sports memories I've had as a player

---

* Barna, *Raising Spiritual Champions.*

and coach, I want to tell you about one that would change my way of life forever.

This particular memory was my personal voice crying in the wilderness—along with thrown bats, helmets, and even a water bottle used as an assault weapon. However, before I get into the personal confessions of that Bobby Knightish period of my career, I want to go back in time and relive some of the greatest sports moments in America (at least, the greatest to me). My son has said I am old and nobody his age, 25, will even know these moments. However, they are etched in my mind and I want to draw on them to remind us of the power of sports and the moments they have provided for generations.

If you are a baseball fan and love baseball history, you may have heard about "the shot heard around the world"—i.e., Bobby Thompson hitting the game-winning home run for the then New York Giants, and the announcer screaming "The Giants win the pennant! The Giants win the pennant!" Or, you may remember "The Catch," with San Francisco 49er Dwight Clark receiving a pass from Joe Montana in the 1981 NFC playoff game in which the 49ers defeated the Dallas Cowboys with 58 seconds remaining on the clock (sorry, Cowboys fans), and then going on to win the Super Bowl a few weeks later.

Another sports moment you may remember, if you are old like me or just a boxing fan, is hearing the distinct voice of Howard Cosell screaming at ringside, "Down goes Frazier! Down goes Frazier!" as Big George Foreman knocked out seemingly unbeatable Joe Frazier. And who can forget Mike Tyson biting off a piece of Evander Holyfield's ear? Tyson bit Holyfield's ear the first time, and, for some reason, the ref decided to let the fight continue. Sure enough, the second bite occurred a few minutes later as the infamous "Bite Fight" became etched in history.

The sports memory that haunts me as a Seattle Seahawks fan was in the late fourth-quarter interception Russell Wilson threw at the goal line in Super Bowl 48 as the hated (by Seattle fans) New England Patriots and Tom Brady won their 100th Super Bowl. (I'm exaggerating, obviously; I really don't hate the Patriots or Tom Brady. I think if you are not from New England, you know what I mean.) But why—why?! Just let Marshawn Lynch run the football!!! As you can tell, it still hurts today. You get a room full of Seahawk fans and mention that play and absolute pandemonium breaks out.

What is it about sports that brings out the absolute best and worst in us as humans? What is it that stirs our emotions to literal tears of sadness and tears of joy? I am a grown man crying when Cal Raleigh hits a home run to send the Seattle Mariners to the playoffs for the first time in 20 years. Why? I guess it touches the depths of my soul. (You will probably want to leave the room if the Mariners ever get to the World Series and win. There may be a tidal wave of tears in the Puget Sound on that glorious day.) The point is that you love your team and you hate your team all in one year. Just listen to your local sports radio show. You love the coaching staff one year; the next year, the fan base is asking for their heads on platters. Al Davis' motto "Just Win, Baby" is the phrase ringing in most of our hearts, if you were to cut us open and look at what truly is inside.

Some of you reading that line may be saying, "I love the 'Just Win, Baby' phrase; what's wrong with that? Are you saying we shouldn't want to win?" Take it easy here; don't pick up stones to hurl at me yet. We will talk later about what "winning" is, according to our particular view of competition. But for now, let's celebrate sports; after all, it is still one of the epic windows that allow us to peer into what is really going on inside of the human heart.

In fact, sports and athletics offer us a tremendous smorgasbord of life opportunities. As you take your tray and head down the sports buffet line, you will have the opportunity to put on your plate the following delicious entrees: success, failure, adversity, critics, believers, unbelievers (as Deion Sanders would say, "Do you believe?"), glory of triumph, agony of defeat, hope—there's always next year (Seattle Mariners Fan ☺)!

If you are reading this book, I know I am preaching to the choir because you have your own memories and your own experiences in your personal world of sports. And, if you are like me, you have been involved in some sort of athletics since you were a kid—as an athlete, coach, parent, fan, or even the thankless job of a referee/umpire. You have had your great experiences, bad experiences, good teammates, bad teammates, good coaches—who were excellent role models for you—and bad coaches whom you would not wish on your worst enemies. You have possibly been on teams or coached teams with incredible parents who seemed like they took the John Wooden course on ethics in sports, and the evil empire parents who continually barrage umpires, coaches, and anyone within earshot. Fortunately, I didn't have too many of the latter in my coaching career. However, the few I did have provided me an abundant supply of opportunities to "bless those who curse you" (Ro. 12:14)!

Invaluable Lessons

The most famous sports moments in history are events we have watched over the years and that we can continue to play through venues like ESPN documentaries. Most of us will never experience sports on the big field, played in front of millions of people. However, our memories from our youth leagues, middle school, high school, and college days are nonetheless big to us. These moments have often been life-shaping and impacting.

I had such a moment in 2005. I was the Head Baseball Coach at a high school in Washington State. Little did I know that this baseball game would be a key factor in changing the way I would approach and think about coaching.

I had grown up as a "Christian Athlete," involved in Fellowship of Christian Athletes in high school and college. We would have Bible studies with some of our Christian coaches and talk about our personal faith. However, I never understood how to integrate faith with my actual playing and coaching during baseball games. Maybe my high school coaches taught us how to integrate our faith and sport and I just wasn't paying attention. Nevertheless, I didn't give much thought to blessing my opponents or umpires. I just wanted to start on my team, do well, win the game, and have great stats.

Now a coach in 2005, I was with my team in the quarterfinals of the State Playoffs. We had won our league championship and sectional playoffs; now we were playing in the Regionals with a chance to go to the Final Four of the Washington State High School Championships.

We found ourselves in a tight ball game that Saturday afternoon. We were playing another great team filled with future Division I players as well as pro prospects. It was a back-and-forth game and we found ourselves down 4–3 going into the last inning, the bottom of the seventh. Our lead-off hitter led off the inning with a single. He advanced to second on a groundout. Our number three hitter walked, putting runners on first and second, with one out.

Our next hitter hit a slow grounder to the shortstop. Our runner on second easily reached third as the shortstop went to second for the force-out. The groundball was hit too softly to turn a double play. However, the second baseman still attempted to complete the double play for the third out, but it wasn't even close as our batter easily beat the throw to first. We were about to have runners on first and third with two outs and our team's leading hitter was coming up to bat.

But then something unbelievable happened! The field umpire looked at our runner sliding into second base and called obstruction on him—which is an automatic out and completion of a double play—and calling the runner at first out as well. Three outs! Game over! Season over!

At this point it was total chaos. Helmets were being thrown, bats were flying, players were yelling, and my first-base coach was kicked out of the game (although it was over). I was in a daze, feeling like I was in a fog as I heard myself yelling, "You can't call that, and end the season that way! I have seniors on the team; it can't end like this!"

Our fans were going crazy. The umpires tried to make a quick exit, fleeing behind the bleachers to the parking lot. Our usually sweet and supportive parents had turned into other beings.

And then came the monumental moment for me. This is the moment that would change my philosophy of coaching and athletics forever. What I am about to say may not seem like a big deal to you. However, to me, it shifted my entire mindset of athletics and the Kingdom of God being displayed (or, rather, *not* being displayed). What occurred is what I, to this day, call "The Water Bottle Assault." The player who had slid into second and was called for obstruction for the game-ending, season-ending double play had a sister who was holding a full water bottle in her hand. As the umpires were running by, she hurled the water bottle at one of them and was on point for a ferocious thud on target. She was a Division I athlete in her own right and I was not surprised by her arm strength and accuracy.

The umpires continued to run to the parking lot but it wasn't over. A group of our fans followed them to the parking lot. With threatening words, one of our fans loudly informed the umpire who had made the call on the field: "I know where you live!" Here is the clincher. That fan who yelled, "I know where you live!" was my sweet, innocent, and loving wife. The sister who threw the on-target water bottle was the daughter of my teaching and coaching colleague, and probably my strongest Christian family. These were ministry people. I was a ministry coach. My first-base coach, the one who was kicked out of the game, was a deacon in his church.

Now, before I sound too judgmental about the water-bottle sister, my wife, myself, or my coach, let me say that I think most people would justify a lot of the anger and emotional outbursts after such a bad call to end a game and season. I think it could be justified that the sister was defending her brother and her love caused her to react with righteous anger (without the throwing of the bottle). It could be said that my wife threatening the umpires with "I know where you live" could be because she loves me so much that she hated to see her beloved husband's team go down in such a fashion. However, the threat was a little weird on telling someone you knew their address. That was a little creepy and maybe going too far.

The Paradigm Shift

After that game, something happened to me. I began to think about myself and how I reacted, and how those I coached had reacted. I knew something wasn't right about the whole scene, and for sure about the scene going on in my heart. If I were truly on a mission to use sports to reach the opponents and even the officials of the game for Christ, wouldn't I have responded differently?

What if our players, fans, and coaches, had all carried the same vision of using sport to reach everyone within our influence and sphere with the gospel and display the Kingdom of Jesus in the midst of great victories and gut-wrenching defeats? I wasn't asking everyone to jump on board with me with the thoughts going on in my mind at that time. But it was the beginning of a different way to look at competition. I was ignorant, which simply means I didn't know what I didn't know. I had not heard of playing and coaching a different way, even as a believer. I had not been exposed to any of the teaching about completing biblically that I was about to experience in the next few years. I had not learned about Frosty Westering's philosophies of competing, Wes Neal's handbook on athletic perfection, or Scotty Kessler's teaching about "competing biblically."

These are all men whom I will talk about later in this book, giants of faith and athleticism who impacted my entire way of thinking about sport. I am grateful for that game in 2005 at some little park in Tacoma, Washington. There were not that many fans and so it is only for a select few of us that it became an infamous sports memory. It was there, in the agony of defeat, that my heart was revealed, and I didn't like what I saw. I saw the opposite of loving my enemy, blessing those that cursed me, doing good to those that hate me, and praying for those that mistreated me.

I wanted more for myself and my coaches and teams, but I had no frame of reference or direction for how to put together a philosophy of coaching and competing that would honor Jesus and still play hard, run the race as if to win, and be a fierce competitor for the glory of God. The only thing I knew was that I loved baseball, I loved Jesus, and I wanted to see athletes and coaches discipled while, at the same time, wanting to coach—during the game—with the mind and attitude of Christ. It was easy for me to pray before and after games, and have Bible studies with athletes. However, *during* games was the issue when things didn't go my way for our team.

By the grace of God, a friend of mine and I started having conversations about reaching athletes for Jesus. He was a wrestling coach and I was a baseball coach. He would have workouts and share the gospel afterwards. I would do the same with baseball. We wanted to disciple athletes and give them great training. But we had no idea how to disciple and definitely didn't know how to teach athletes how to compete to the glory of God. We loved Jesus and relied on Him to show us what to do.

Over the next few chapters, I would like to take you on the journey I embarked on, the one where I began to use sport and quit letting it use me. I am still a work in progress and to this day regularly have to put my flesh to death in the area of wanting *my* will to be done and not His. I am grateful to have had the opportunity to come under the teaching of Scotty Kessler and his teachings on competing biblically. It not only changed my coaching but has also leaked into all the areas of my life. My marriage has been impacted, as have been my work/job responsibilities, parenting, ministry, and relationships.

I hope you enjoy the journey and remain open. Maybe you do not have a "voice crying in the wilderness" experience exactly like mine that includes water-bottle tossing and threats against umpires, but I bet you do have milestones that led you to wanting to become the best coach, player, or spectator you can become to the glory of God.

As my mentor and co-author, Scotty Kessler, says, "We all stand on the shoulders of those who have gone before us." Whose shoulders are you standing on? I invite you to stand on the shoulders of this particular philosophy of sport. As you explore the following pages in this book, you may not agree with everything we believe in. That is okay, as there are a lot of philosophies of competition out there. We will never declare that our philosophy of competing biblically is the only godly way; it is just the best way for us. We would just encourage you to have a philosophy that is biblical and will enhance the Kingdom of God. I would encourage you to be a FATC person as you read: be Faithful, Available, Teachable, and Courageous.

The intention of this book is to help you create a plan to use sport for evangelism and discipleship. It is our desire that you will have this book as a resource to be a part of raising up an army of athletes and coaches that equip future and current fathers, mothers, employers, and employees to expand the Kingdom of God using the platform of sports.

Our goal is for you to:

Have a plan . . .

. . . make it a good plan

. . . and execute the plan.

Discussion Questions

1. Can you think of a time in your own sports journey when your faith or values were tested in competition?

2. What does it mean to "compete biblically" in sports, and how does this contrast with the typical win-at-all-costs mindset often seen in athletics?"

3. Nelson Mandela said, "Sport has the power to unite people in a way that little else does." How can coaches and athletes

intentionally use this unifying power of sport to build relationships and share the gospel?

4. Given that a person's worldview is largely shaped by age 13, what opportunities do we have as coaches, mentors, or leaders to disciple young athletes through sport? What does intentional discipleship look like on a field, court, or gym?

5. The 2005 game story illustrates how sports can expose what's truly in our hearts. What have sports revealed in your heart—both good and bad? How can we allow those moments to shape us more into the image of Christ?

CHAPTER 2

WHOSE SHOULDERS ARE YOU STANDING ON?

"Each of us stand on the shoulders of others.
The question is not if we stand on shoulders, but
whose shoulders are we standing on?"
—Scotty Kessler

Competing biblically is the integration of sport and faith. The guts of the philosophy are built on four ideas:

1. How we treat the scoreboard
2. How we treat the opponent
3. How we treat the officials
4. How we compete during games

Before we get into the nuts and bolts of what that looks like and how we create a personal plan to accomplish it, I'd like to back up and establish for readers just exactly what is the history and legacy of the *Competing Biblically* philosophy.

All philosophies have an origin. Your ideas and thoughts come from not only some*place* but some*one*. This is why it is of utmost importance that you choose wisely whose shoulders you are standing on. With that in mind, what is *your* philosophy of competition as a coach or athlete?

Is it a biblical approach to sport? From where did you develop your philosophy? Whose shoulders are you standing on in the area of your coaching or playing philosophy?

Most coaches will approach their own coaching style based on what they learned from their own experience. In the athletic world, we call this a "coaching tree." In the church world, we call this discipleship. The fact of the matter is that you will more than likely adopt a philosophy of competing and coaching from those under whom you played or coached. It may not look exactly the same in your own coaching style, but you will take on the traits of those you with whom you spent countless hours on the field or in the gym.

However, if you were never introduced to a biblical approach to competition, it is not too late. I did not hear (even as a Christian athlete) a "competing biblically" approach until six years into my coaching career. I competed as a Christian athlete growing up but never had the faintest idea that I could use sport as a way to display the Kingdom of God.

There are two revered coaches on whose shoulders the *Competing Biblically* philosophy rests: Wes Neal and Frosty Westering. For many of us, the lives and careers of these two coaches paved the way for our way of competing and living our lives.

Beginning in the late 60s and early 70s, Wes talked about the integration of sport and faith in a way that had not been publicly discussed before, making him one of the early pioneers of the current sports ministry movement, a philosophy of competition he first articulated in a book called *The Handbook on Athletic Perfection*. The fruit of this groundbreaking book, which was written almost 50 years ago, can be seen in numerous sports ministries in the USA and internationally.

In the early 1970s, Wes was a part of the Athletes in Action weightlifting team. One day, while he was lifting at their headquarters in Southern California, pulling the weight, he squatted under it to catch the bar on his front deltoids, and it went off balance. To avoid being pinned, Wes pushed himself away from the bar. As the weight thumped in front of him, he fell backwards and slammed his hand on the platform in anger.

All of the lifters stopped and looked at him, the so-called model for being a Christian athlete. Wes felt embarrassed when he saw his fellow athletes incredulously watching his fit of rage. It was at that moment he realized there was no difference between how he reacted to failure as a Christian and how he reacted as a non-believer.

Later that day, in reliving the incident in his mind, Wes told God that he would take steps in leaning into how He wanted him to lift weights. And that's when he started to go through the New Testament, writing down any verses he could find that correlated to sport. He soon had numerous stacks of three-by-five cards—cards that would eventually become the chapters of *The Handbook on Athletic Perfection*.

I am proud to know Wes personally, and he told me that he did not start out with a book in mind—that he had been the one in need of a book! I am grateful for his humility and willingness to believe the gospel within sports and for giving the world a masterpiece of writing on this topic from the Master Himself. I am actually glad that Wes slammed his hand in anger that day. This began his soul-searching journey to discover how his relationship with Jesus should play out during his lifting.

We can never realize the fruit of one man's journey. I seriously doubt that Wes Neal had any idea that his personal efforts would lead to a book that impacted my mentor, Scotty Kessler, and would catapult Kess's ministry of 40-plus years in coaching and discipleship. Scotty Kessler was 16 when his mom gave him a copy of *The Handbook on Athletic Perfection*. The impact on Kess was transformative.

Kess said the following about his encounter with the book:

> *My life was changed through the Holy Spirit by my encounter with* The Handbook on Athletic Perfection. *In my teen years, I read this book without a human walking me through it; the Holy Spirit was so much in its pages that it connected the dots*

for me. I was sincerely trying to follow Jesus as a teenager and I loved playing sports. Sport was connection with life to me; I loved it passionately. I did love God, but I didn't understand the integration of my faith with my play.

The Holy Spirit taught me through the book that sport and faith were congruent, that they were meant to be together, and that the Holy Spirit wanted to infuse them together in me. One of the metaphors Wes Neal used was that, if I had a white glove and I held it up, it would be limp. But if you put a hand into the glove, then that glove with the hand inside it could play beautiful music. It could do things that the glove alone had no ability to do.

In a sense, we are all like that glove. In the Scriptures, the Apostle Paul compared us to "jars of clay" (2 Cor. 4:7), with the Spirit of God inside of us. He wants to work through us—in our words, in our deeds, in our attitudes, in every way. He wants to infuse us so we can play and coach what we call, in *Competing Biblically*, "To-By-For":

According TO His Word, BY His power, FOR the glory of God.

We can all compete To-By-For. As a high school kid, I had no idea about any of this. I just knew that I'd ask God to help me, or give me a good game, or help us win. At the end of a game, I thanked Him either a lot or not at all, depending on how it played out. All of that is twisted. It's less than elementary school. It's an uninformed thought about how sport and life are integrated.

Life and faith are to be integrated. The way we approach sport, when we do it in ignorance and blindness, is how we live. We go to church on Sunday, we pray at a meal, and Jesus may have no part practically in our day, but we are sincere about God. We love God; we would consider Him our first love, we really would, but you wouldn't see that in the impact because we're like everybody else.

In the same way, an athlete may be serious about God, but if he doesn't understand the integration of life and faith, he's going to play just like the world. He is going to play like the world and talk like the world, even though it may be seasoned with some grace. Fundamentally, that philosophy is still not driven by the Spirit of God. It may be driven by a noble desire to want God to be present, but it would not be the hand-in-glove scenario we are talking about.

For me, when I ran across *The Handbook on Athletic Perfection*, God gave me a moment of revelation that transformed my thinking. It changed me from a guy that sport was using to a guy who was using sport to advance the Kingdom, even at an elementary level. Wes Neal was, for many, one of the benchmark framers of the integration of sport and faith in a document that people could chew on and play out.

Of course, the tricky part is just that: playing it out. In my own coaching circles, we often talk about "the What, the Why, and the How." The How will always be where the rubber meets the road. It is complicated because Satan wants to be glorified and God wants to be glorified. Therein lies the battle between light and darkness that shows up in competing, which is driven significantly by pride, ego, fear of failure, and fear of what people think. It is in this very visible battlefield that sport is extremely educational in revealing to us our hearts and how we live out the Great Commission lifestyle on the field.

The Second Set of Giant Shoulders: Frosty Westering

The second giant on whose shoulders the *Competing Biblically* philosophy rests was Coach Frosty Westering. Frosty coached football for 51 years (32 of those years at Pacific Lutheran University in Tacoma, Washington) and left a legacy that went far beyond his 305 wins and four national championships. He was inducted as a member of five Halls of Fame, and received numerous Lifetime Achievement Awards. In the recently published book, *I Played for Frosty*, 134 of Frosty's former athletes tell about the impact Frosty had on their lives, spanning from 1952 to 2003.

Frosty created a classic acronym during his coaching days at PLU. Pacific Lutheran's mascot was called a "Lute" and Frosty came up with EMAL, meaning "Every Man A Lute." This phrase was used to help people "buy in" to a philosophy that was very different from possibly any program in the country. It was based upon celebrating the day, your teammates, your commitment to them, and the joy of being on the "success road," which was distinctly different than the "road to success." EMAL involved every mom, dad, brother, sister, and friend who was involved in the program. Being an EMAL truly made people feel part of something bigger than themselves.

Frosty was the only child in a family that loved sports and played sports. He went to the Marines and saw sports through the Marine vehicle, and came out with the recognition that the mentality of blood and guts, win and dominate, was the way people approach sports even today. He also came out of the Marines believing there had to be a different way to play and coach.

Scotty Kessler had the opportunity to play for—and later coach with—Frosty at PLU. He describes his time with Frosty:

> My experience with Frosty—as someone who played both with and under him—was he, like Wes Neal, had what I would call the genius of God to see something differently, at least in our generation, than other people were seeing it, and to articulate it. Wes Neal was a concept and Frosty was someone who lived it out."
>
> For me, the start of Competing Biblically was Wes Neal; he was the beginning of the thought of the integration of sport and faith. He took me from reading a book to starting some application, changing the way I thought and the way I performed. But the practical outworking of that was in the context

of playing with someone, Frosty Westering, who really drove the philosophy of competing biblically. It was his philosophy.

Of course, each of us stands on the shoulders of others. The question is not *if* we stand on the shoulders of others, but *whose* shoulders we are standing on. I stand on the shoulders of Wes Neal and Frosty Westering. These two individuals will be alluded to throughout the book. We will particularly refer frequently to Frosty Westering because so much of who Scotty Kessler is, and the articulation of this philosophy, comes from what Kess heard and saw from Frosty, and from the full playing out of "Frostyisms" for a decade of almost-daily interactions with him within the sport context.

Another excellent description of Frosty's impact on thousands of lives was in an article written by Jason Bevens in SB Nation—Field Gulls:

> *I had the distinct pleasure of playing baseball for Pacific Lutheran University, an experience I'll treasure forever. But when their legendary football coach Frosty Westering announced, going into my junior year, that it would be his final season, I took advantage of the unique opportunity to try and walk on to the team. I had seen the transformative effect Frosty had had on some of my closest friends who played for him, and I wanted to be a part of it.*
>
> *The next four months had a profound impact on me. I saw a coach lead with his heart, put others before self, and emphasize the fun of playing football to a degree that was unimaginable until I experienced it first-hand. It was pure servant leadership, a team hyper-focused on making each other better and the absolute elimination of personal ego. And we won a lot of games. Frosty retired as the ninth winningest college football coach in history (12th as of 2024)—at any level. He led his team to 261 victories, four national championships, was the National Coach of the Year three times, and was inducted into*

the College Football Hall of Fame in 2005. He enlarged the hearts of everyone lucky enough to play for him, talking about being the best person you could be more than he did football.

That autumn changed my life, even though I was at the absolute bottom of the depth chart. And when it was over, I wanted to believe that his approach could work on a bigger stage than Division III football. I wanted to believe that joy wasn't just a reaction to success but the cause of it, that the highest heights of a brutal sport could be reached on the twin engines of fun and competition.

What (or Who) Shapes Your Practices?

As a coach, player, parent, or fan, it is essential to recognize that your approach to competition, coaching, and parenting is influenced by others. It begs the question: what or who is shaping your practices and beliefs? By referencing Wes Neal and Frosty Westering here, we highlight the importance of understanding that our belief and value systems are formed by what we absorb and integrate into our daily lives. Sports provide a platform for coaches, athletes, and parents to demonstrate their character.

As my former pastor frequently mentioned, we are akin to sponges—what emerges under pressure reveals our core. The athletic field remains an excellent arena to observe such character under stress. So, it is crucial to comprehend whose influence you are under. Your approach to sport and life will be directly related to those shoulders.

Choose wisely where you stand. Choose men and women who have ultimately stood on the shoulders of the Word of God and live that out consistently. We believe it would be wise if, as a parent, you surround your children with men and women who have a solid foundation on the Rock, Christ Jesus. At the end of the day, it will never be about anything but the foundation of Jesus and His Word.

Discussion Questions

1. Take a moment to honestly assess how you coach or compete. What is your competition philosophy as a coach or athlete?
   - Is it driven by outcomes (wins/losses, stats, accolades)?
   - Is it driven by growth (character, effort, learning, relationships)?
   - Is it driven by a deeper purpose (glorifying God, serving others, eternal impact)?

2. Is your philosophy of competition aligned with biblical principles? Why or why not?
   - Do you see your sport as an act of worship?
   - Does your treatment of opponents, teammates, officials, and the scoreboard reflect the fruits of the Spirit?
   - Do you play/coach To-By-For: TO His Word, BY His power, FOR His glory?

3. Where did your philosophy originate?
   - Who were the most influential coaches, athletes, or mentors in your life?
   - What lessons—spoken or unspoken—did they pass down to you about competition and character?
   - Have you ever intentionally examined or questioned those influences?

4. Who influenced your coaching or playing philosophy?
   - Were you shaped by a "win-at-all-costs" mentor, or someone like Frosty who celebrated joy, humility, and team?
   - Have you had a "Wes Neal moment"—a turning point where God used an experience to reveal something deeper about your approach?
   - Are there voices in your life today helping you align more closely with Christ-centered competition?

CHAPTER 3

COMPETING FROM THE CORRECT TREE

*"Competing biblically is not something you do. It's some-
one you become. It's someone you are. This is integrated so it's not just performance.
It's an external manifestation of an inward transformation."*
—Scotty Kessler

*"All of us come from one of the two trees in the history of man. We
either come from the Tree of Rebellion, of which Adam and Eve
ate, OR we come from the Tree of the Cross, where Jesus paid the
penalty of sin. Unfortunately, we were born attached to the Tree of
Adam (Rebellion). However, all glory to Jesus that we can attach
ourselves to His Tree through His shed blood upon the tree. "*
—Tim Kuykendall

*"I am the way, the truth, and the life. No one
comes to the Father except through me."*
—Jesus Christ in John 14:6

Wes Neal calls the fruit of the Spirit in Galatians 5:22–23 the
"Nine Attitudes of the Athlete." Imagine playing, coaching, or

observing sport with Love, Joy, Peace, Patience, Kindness, Goodness, Gentleness, Faithfulness, and Self-Control. I know I want that for my coaching and playing pickleball (pickleball gets intense, by the way). Imagine playing with a whole heart, a clear mind, a strong will, and a great passion. Is it possible to play with these attitudes? We 100 percent believe it is possible. However, there is the old nature from our great, great, great, great, great . . . granddad, Adam.

We were all born from Adam and our first instinct will always be to attach ourselves to the old way of thinking. Our sin and rebellion were redeemed at the cross of Christ. Galatians 2:20 says, "I have been crucified with Christ and I no longer live but Christ lives in me, the life I live in the body I live by faith in the son of God who loved me and gave himself for me." However, in my own life, and the lives of many other believers whom I have seen attempting to play sports, I see how we tend to think according to the flesh, with all its emotions that are involved in sport.

In *Competing Biblically*, we use the phrase "To-By-For" to reiterate that we are truly living according TO what the Bible declares about our identity in Jesus. We live BY faith in the Son of God who loved us and gave Himself FOR us. This is another take on the phrase To-By-For—to emphasize that we are of Christ. Yes, we were born into Adam and inherited the sin nature of Adam, BUT we are now in Christ and no longer have to live, coach, play, or parent from that nature. We no longer have to have fear, anxiety, hatred, confusion, pride, or jealousy. These are all fruits from the Adam Tree. We come from the Jesus Tree.

Let's talk about identity here for a moment. There are two sides here

1. We were born into Adam—our natural minds are set on the flesh (Ro. 8:5a).
2. We must be born again—our mind is set on the Spirit once we are born again. (John 3:16. Ro. 8:5b). Flesh gives birth to flesh; spirit gives birth to spirit (John 3:6).

DNA From Adam:	DNA From Jesus:
Unbelief	Belief
Disunity	Unity
Unsubmission to authority	Submission to authority
Pride	Humility
Selfishness	SelfLESSness

How might our emotions from Adam (i.e., anger, fear, jealousy, hate, arrogance, etc.) integrate into our sports competition and life? Is it possible that many of our thoughts, ideas, and philosophies about competition come from the wrong Tree? The answer is yes, one hundred percent, yes! The Apostle Paul called it a good fight of faith (1 Timothy 6:12). This is the battle. This is why we teach and preach the To-By-For concept with *Competing Biblically*.

By definition, *Competing Biblically* is a philosophy of competition integrating sport and faith whose primary purpose is to glorify God and advance His Kingdom to reach the world with the gospel through the vehicle of sport. It's not simply a playing philosophy or a coaching philosophy.

We believe that sport is a powerful tool that can be used to shape gospel thinking in every aspect of our lives. We talk about displaying the Kingdom of God to the world, but we also believe that sports played and coached as an act of worship to God transform the heart and mind of the individual athlete and coach. In fact, parents and spectators as well can be transformed when participating in sports through the filter of worship and bringing glory to God. We believe this philosophy is a lifestyle. We call it the Great Commission Lifestyle.

"To-By-For"

Under this philosophy of sport, both player and coach alike fall under the umbrella of To-By-For. That means "According TO the Word of

God, BY the power of God, FOR the glory of God. When we speak of To-By-For, that's what we are alluding to throughout the book:

1. According TO the Word of God

This means the Word of God is the filter. If it doesn't run through the filter, if it isn't biblically supportable, then it is off limits, even if it's practically "helpful." For example, if someone thinks they have to be angry and hate their opponent to motivate themselves to perform better, we would consider that unbiblical because it would not pass muster with the Word of God. Thus, even if it has some translatable outcome that's positive, it is not acceptable or allowable in the context of our philosophy.

I realize this goes against many of the philosophies of competition that most of us grew up with. I remember when I was 11 and our Pop Warner football coaches gave us our pre-game speech before our championship game in the great state of Texas. (Football truly is King in Texas). Our team name was the Eagles.

One of our coaches held in his hand a bag of birdseed as he began his speech about how the opposing teams' coaches had placed the bag of birdseed by our bench, insinuating that we were just birdseed. I guess we figured that was bad, in our 11-year-old minds, as our coaches were attempting to fire us up with anger at the opponent to increase our level of play. Looking back, the bag of bird seed would be positive for a bunch of birds, but nonetheless, we were being taught to use anger as fuel. I guess it worked, as we trounced our opponent 40–0.

We are not saying hate and anger don't work as motivational forces. Look at Michael Jordan and the pent-up anger he would use to his advantage. There are locker rooms full of opposing teams' negative and disrespectful comments made by some players to the press and now plastered on the wall as motivation. But let's not mix up that kind of anger with righteous anger, like Jesus in the temple, or David fearing and loving the God of Israel and having righteous anger towards

Goliath. We can't compare that to the anger of youth coaches putting birdseed by our bench!

This philosophy of competition relies on the Word of God as the boundary line. There are a lot of things that happen that are not covered in the Word of God, but we are looking at principles that are translatable to the sports context. We will address those principles throughout this book, using the Word of God as our filter.

2. BY the power of God

"By the power of God" is saying that this is not a philosophy that relies on the power of man's (or woman's) ability to play or perform. It is impossible, apart from the Holy Spirit, to compete biblically. The word "compete," from the original Latin form of the word, meant to strive with and not against. It was not somebody you were trying to beat; it was somebody you were partnering with. That was the original design as we understand it from antiquity. We see this as biblical and hope to emulate that in our play and coaching.

Romans 3:23 says, "For all have sinned and fall short of the glory of God." Our natural human bent is selfishness, ego, and exalting ourselves. Our natural bent is to increase. The Scriptures say *He* must increase, and we must decrease (John 3:30). That's really only going to happen by the Holy Spirit. All aspects of sport, if not driven by the Holy Spirit, are going to be fractured and flawed. We move back and forth between our will and His will, wanting our will and wanting to win versus wanting His will. It's impossible to pull this philosophy off in a regular consistent way without the power of the Holy Spirit permeating it. That doesn't mean in every instance someone is going to be driven by the Holy Spirit. It just means this is the target—and it's possible. Second Peter 1:3 says, "God has given us everything we need for life and godliness."

The source of power for this philosophy is the Holy Spirit and BY His power. Second Timothy 1:7 says, "For God has not given you a spirit of fear but of power, love, and self-discipline" (NIV). You don't have to be afraid of failing. You don't have to seek the approval of others. God has filled you with His love. In fact, the Scriptures say that God is love. You can love the sport you play. You can love your teammates. And you can have self-discipline and a sound mind while you're participating in sport.

3. FOR the Glory of God

"For the glory of God" emphasizes the part about "He must increase and we must decrease" (John 3:30). This is for His glory: His will, His Word, His way, the process, and the outcomes. It's all-encompassing. It's a lifestyle—the Great Commission Sports Lifestyle. It bleeds over and through every aspect of our lives.

Our testimony is that whenever we had a revelation from the Word of God about how the Holy Spirit wanted to play and coach through us, according TO His Word, BY His Power, and FOR His glory, it was a game changer. It transformed our way of thinking and not just in the sport context. It gave us an applicable structure of how to think about life, how to live in the Spirit and for His glory.

When we talk about the integration of sport and faith, we're talking about something for which sport is the vehicle for education that translates into a transformed lifestyle. Like we see in Romans 12:2, this philosophy renews our mind: "Do not be conformed to this world, but be transformed by the renewal of your mind, that by testing you may discern what is the will of God, what is good and acceptable and perfect" (ESV). It causes us to think differently. It makes us somebody who processes through the lens of the Word of God by His power and for His glory, instead of somebody who is thinking about our own want or desire.

I have to pause here and tell you about an experience I had with Scotty Kessler when it came to competing To-By-For. I had the privilege of coaching baseball with Kess one summer as our sons were playing together on a faith-based baseball team named Reality Sports. I was the co-founder of Reality Sports and was already being mentored and discipled by Kess in the *Competing Biblically* philosophy. We were close to starting the game and Kess wanted to pray with the team. I had prayed with Kess numerous times but this particular prayer rocked my thinking about the actual process of the game.

Kess started the prayer with the typical thankfulness for the ability to physically play the game with the gifts and talents we had been given. Then, with authority, he prayed, "And Lord, if it's Your will that we get our teeth kicked in by our opponent today—for whatever reason, You want us to lose and them to win—then Your will be done! Not our will, but Your will be done. We will give it our best shot and play for Your glory, but Your plan is bigger than our plan."

He got louder and louder as he continued, "We want Your will! Your will! Your will!" And then ended it with a confident, "Amen!" I was taken aback by the prayer. Of course, I thought I wanted God's will for the game, but I don't think I had ever committed a game to Him with the fervency or faith that Kess's prayer had brought. I realized that I thought I wanted His will but I also wanted to win the game if at all possible. My pre-game prayers of keeping everyone safe, enjoying the game of baseball, and displaying the Kingdom of God (which is a good prayer, I think) still had a hint of "and help us win if possible" in it. I don't think I had truly considered what "for His glory" meant until that prayer.

I am grateful for the fervency of Kess's prayer. There was nothing soft about it. If I had just heard about a prayer like that, I may have dismissed it as a soft approach to competing. But to actually hear the prayer in person and feel the depths of the meaning behind it was, to me, similar to Jesus' prayer in the Garden of Gethsemane: "Not My will but Your will be done" (Luke 22:42). The prayer Kess prayed that day freed me up to coach To-By-For during that game and many games after. I believe it also helps the players feel free to just go play for His will to be done. His will to be done *is* His Glory. I must admit that I have often relied heavily upon "By His Power" to get to the "For His Glory" part of my coaching and living. At the end of the day, it is a beautiful sequence of playing, coaching, and living a To-By-For lifestyle.

Scriptural Foundations of the TO-BY-FOR Philosophy

Competing "according TO the Word of God," then, will be the base foundation to this philosophy. As such, we want to give you some of the verses that have influenced us in our way of thinking in regards to our playing and coaching—our Verse Bank for *Competing Biblically.*

1 Corinthians 10:31

". . . Whether you eat or drink, or whatever you do, do it for the glory of God" (ESV). The "whatever you do" part encapsulates hitting a baseball, making a tackle, lifting weights, etc.—all of these are acts of worship we can perform to His glory.

Colossians 3:17

"Whatever you do, in word or deed, do everything in the name of the Lord Jesus, giving thanks to God the Father through him" (ESV). Be thankful for what He's done. Create a culture of thanksgiving before, during, and after competition regardless of performance or result. It is all to His glory.

Colossians 1:28

"He is the one we proclaim, We proclaim Him and not ourselves. It is not about us but about Jesus being glorified" (my paraphrase). Think about the world's philosophy: it's about #1; it's about making a big play; it's about drawing attention to yourself; it's about provoking your opponent. All of these are counterintuitive to our distinctiveness. It's *His* power, *His* Word, *His* glory. That doesn't mean we don't play a part. We bring our five loaves and two fish. Bring your best shot every moment; give everything you have at that moment, with that practice rep or that game rep or that workout. In season or off season, big game or small game, or practice, whatever it is, give it your best effort, for the glory of God at that moment. Proclaim Him with your play.

This approach is pounded repeatedly in *The Athletic Handbook* by Wes Neal. We play our part. We exercise our will. It's the doctrine of both. Is it Him or is it you? The answer is yes. It's a co-mission. We play together. It's us and it's Him in us—playing through us, living through us. We die to ourselves. When we say, "Not my will but Yours be done," He plays beautiful music through us, not compared to others, not compared to the world.

We close the gap—Frosty's terminology—between our potential, which is a gift from God that is different for everybody, and our performance. Our performance gap closes as we die to ourselves and allow Him to play and live through us, when we're not resistant to the Holy Spirit. That's the battle. That's where we "work out our salvation in fear and trembling" (Philippians 2:12) in our life and in our play.

Ecclesiastes 9:10

"Whatever your hand finds to do, do it with all your might." This is full-effort, fire-breathing, hair-on-fire effort. We should play with a ferocity and all our might.

Colossians 3:23

"Work at it with all your heart." This is where we get the term "whole-hearted." Competing biblically is working with your whole heart for the Lord, in order to receive an inheritance. This inheritance is invisible. It's about eternity. Your target is *eternity*. Our home is heaven and we are strangers here. Earth is not our home. Our life is not our own. These are foundational core values.

People may think we are just talking about football, basketball, or baseball. No, we're talking about eternity. We are talking about the Kingdom of light versus the kingdom of darkness. These are the things that are on our minds all the time. This is the target, and we have to make sure we stay on track for it. If you get onto a different track, it's not going to hit the target. If you're off even one percent, and you play it out, you're completely separate. That's why it is so critical we know who we are, our identity in Jesus: what we believe, where our home is, where our power is, whom we're playing for and why. All these things have to be articulated as a foundational core starting point so that we have a chance, once we get on the playing field, to hit the target. All bets are off once you get on the grass.

Unfortunately, I know this to be true about my heart being exposed once I stepped onto the field and the scoreboard flipped on. I, as a Jesus confessor, particularly in my youth, in ignorance, was about my power and my glory and whatever philosophy was popular that day. I certainly didn't implement biblical principles in a lot of my play—not because I didn't want to, but because I didn't know how to integrate it. I know I am not alone in this; thus, we have developed this philosophy we are attempting to share in a To-By-For model to help people think about sport in terms of Scripture.

1 Corinthians 9:24–25

"Do you not know that in a race all the runners run, but only one gets the prize? Run in such a way as to get the prize. Everyone who competes in the games goes into strict training. They do it to get a crown that will not last, but we do it to get a crown that will last forever."

This passage isn't about winning the temporary prize; it is about a crown in eternity. This is, once again, invisible. The prize is not winning. The prize is not the scoreboard. It's not a primary goal or even a secondary goal. It's a byproduct that we leave in the hands of God. Now, that alone is different than the world's philosophy and it's going to cause separation. Just like with Jesus, they loved the miracles, but when He started talking about the cost and death and dying to self, people started stepping away. Finally, it got to a point where He said to His disciples, "Are you going to leave also?"

And Peter replied, "To whom shall we go? You have the words of eternal life" (John 6:68). That's how we feel about *Competing Biblically*. What other philosophy is there, besides this one, that is according TO the Word of God, BY the power of God, FOR the glory of God? The prize is eternity and everything has to be on that target.

We agree to disagree with all people who confess Jesus' name who have a philosophy that is a little (or a lot) different from ours, in particular how they treat the scoreboard-winning and losing, and how they treat the opponent and referees. There can be tremendous disagreement about that. But we need not be disagreeable even if we disagree on concept and practice. It all tends to show up on game day as our hearts open up and our attitude toward winning and losing is tested.

Philosophies are nice in classroom settings. Games are where the rubber meets the road and you rub the flesh in terms of individuals' own desires, goals, and agendas. Is it about our will or God's will? Whose will do we want done? What is the process like?

The result may appear to be successful, but if the process is unbiblical, it doesn't matter what the end is. The end and the means must be biblical.

Discussion Questions

1. Which "tree" are you competing from more—Adam or Christ?
   - How can you determine if your motivations and responses in competition are rooted in the flesh or in the Spirit?
   - What might it practically look like to shift your identity from performance-based to Christ-based?

2. How does the Fruit of the Spirit shape your athletic or coaching mindset?
   - Which of the "Nine Attitudes of the Athlete" is hardest for you to live out in competitive moments?
   - How can these fruits actually enhance—not weaken—your intensity and focus?
3. What does it mean to compete "BY the power of God"?
   - When you're exhausted, angry, or pressured, how can you rely on the Spirit instead of self?
   - Can you think of a time when God empowered you to respond differently than you normally would in a competitive situation?
4. Are you truly competing FOR the glory of God—or for something else?
   - Whose approval matters most to you after a win or a loss?
   - What would change if every game, practice, and workout was worship?

SECTION 2

The TO-BY-FOR Foundation

CHAPTER 4

THE 6 OVERS OF COMPETING BIBLICALLY

*"Everyone then who hears these words of mine and does them will
be like a wise man who built his house upon the rock. And the rain
fell, and the floods came, and the winds blew and beat on that
house, but it did not fall, because it had been founded on the rock."*
—Matthew 7:24–25

Hearing and doing are key within the *Competing Biblically* philosophy. We are praying for this wisdom to fill our hearts because we know that "rain, floods, and wind" are in the forecast for most teams and sports. "In this world you will have trouble," Jesus said to His disciples (John 16:33). If we know the rain is coming, we need to dig deep and lay the foundation that has been provided for us according TO His Word, BY His power, and FOR His Glory.

It is fascinating to read how deep the foundations are that support some of the tallest buildings in the world. The foundations of the Empire State Building are 55 feet, eight inches. The height of the Empire State Building is 1,250 feet (381 m). The entire steel framework that supports the Empire State Building, in accordance with the construction criteria of the time, is covered with concrete and bricks. The total weight of the building is estimated to be 365,000 tons, resting on foundations made up of 210 pillars.[*]

The current tallest towers in the world are the Petronas Towers in Malaysia. As of 2022, their foundations remained the world's deepest, coming in at 400 feet deep. The height of the Petrona Towers is 1,483 feet (452 meters); the depths of their foundations are crucial for their survival and existence. Without the foundations, these buildings would collapse in a catastrophic event.

Similarly, the foundations in our lives have to go deep to withstand whatever may come against our house. As coaches and leaders on our teams, we have to keep pouring the concrete and build pillars that will support the generations to come.

Building on Solid Foundations

Have you ever played on or coached a team that seemed to have a house that was built on the sand? Any sort of adversity and some of the people on the team would collapse. There was a team in our league that was super talented most years, but we knew if we could get to them early, they would quit or not fight their way through the ebbs and flows of the game. Part of the reason for this was that their coach would freak out anytime someone made a mistake or a call went against their team. You could see it coming with their demeanor and could predict the collapse. This team's foundation was built on false expectations, fear of failure, and selfishness. It was actually sad to watch.

On the other hand, have you been on a team or competed against a team that always showed up to play their guts out? You knew the game would be hard fought as the foundation of the team was rock solid. It didn't matter what kind of adversity hit or what call went

---

* Quora.com, October 14, 2020, Accessed April 1, 2025.

against that team; their resilience was contagious and made the game enjoyable and fierce.

For this second scenario to become a reality, it all starts with the leadership of the coaches as well as team leaders. Is it possible to be completely storm proof as an organization as you build its foundation? Yes, according to the words of Jesus Himself. Describing the house built on the rock, He said, "that house did not fall." He acknowledged there would be wind, rain, and floods. But He also promised that the house would stand if we would hear His words AND do them.

The Foundations (The 6 Overs)

The Foundations—or what some in our network call "The 6 Overs"—of *Competing Biblically* will prepare us to remain standing after the storm subsides. We may be a little wet, but we will still be standing. Here are the Principles of the 6 Overs:

Principle #1—Team over the Individual

Jesus was the ultimate team player. He put the team (the people of the world) before Himself. We know from Philippians 2:7 that He humbled Himself, that He didn't grasp for His power as God although He was God. He didn't use His power for His selfishness; but in humility, He emptied Himself for our sake, the sake of the Team.

In the Greek and Roman world of gods and goddesses, this was a foreign concept. The deities of that culture came to Earth for their selfish gain or to settle a score with someone or something. Jesus, as God, gave everything up for the sake of others. Can you imagine playing on a team with players and coaches possessing that mindset? The crazy thing is that Jesus asks us to *follow* Him. We are actually supposed to do the same thing He did while on Earth. Put the team before your individual needs. Give your life away as an individual for the sake of the team.

John Wooden said, "When an individual chooses to be part of a team, he ceases to exist as an individual." Of course, everyone is still an individual. We still have our individual personality traits. However, in comparison to the team, it is as *if* you don't exist as an individual. We like to reference a Bible verse in discipleship that says, "Unless you hate father, brother, sister, or mother for the sake of Christ, you have no part of Him" (Luke 14:26–30).

Does that mean you're going to literally hate them? No! The Bible talks about loving others more than yourself. However, compared to your love for God, it is as if you don't love them at all. It's a rhetorical device known as hyperbole, a way to contrast and compare. God is trying to say that you need to love Him more than your closest friends and family members.

In a similar way, we love competing. We exist as individuals. But compared to the team, it is as *if* we don't exist at all. The team matters more than the individual. And if I'm the head coach, what matters is the team. The head coach is part of the team and great coaches lead by putting the program first.

There are different roles on every team. We talk about the team over the individual; it's not the cessation of the individual. Each individual is still a unique person whom we care about deeply. But in the climate and culture of competing biblically, the individual submits to the goal of the team. The individual says, "Not my will, but yours be done." In an ideal scenario, the player is going to say something like, "I like to catch, but if there's a better scenario that's better for the team, that's what I want. If you want me to start, that's what I want. If you want me to be back up, that's what I want." This is the way this philosophy plays itself out on the court or on the field. You have people from the bottom up putting the team over their own individual needs.

Great teammates always say the team is more important than themselves. It's fundamental in sports and organization as well as in the Kingdom of God.

Principle #2—Long Term over Short Term

When we talk about-long term over short-term, we are thinking about eternity and working backwards. Here is something we often say to our players: "You're thinking about this year or your career, but you're only going to be here four years. I'm going to be here hypothetically 10, 20, or 30 years. We're making decisions about the program. When you've stopped playing, you're still part of the program; you just have a different role—you're an alumnus." My hope is that if I do a good job as a head coach, the players will feel like they are part of the program after they leave.

We will always include former athletes in the program and intend for the program to continue for a long time. The best programs have history, legacy, and tradition. Keep people involved in the sequence after their playing days; that's how you develop a culture of family and tradition. It's an extended family that lasts for generations. That's why you have to think about the organization as a *program* and not just a team. This is about the team, not about the individual. This is about decades of family structure, not just about this little window of time. In fact, if the head coach leaves, if the Athletic Director is bought in, someone can take over who shares the program's convictions and values. Our goal is to work ourselves out of a job!

The same is true of a father and mother in a family. At some point, the parents are going to die. Children are going to take over the family's legacy. The hope of all God-fearing parents is that their children and their children's children will continue to worship Jesus and make disciples. This is the target we are aiming for.

Does it always play out perfectly? No, sometimes not. But these are the targets and goals of our teams. If you don't have a target, you're not going to hit it. Our objective is the long term over the short term. It's over the span of a lifetime.

We have an answer for people when they ask us, "How did your season go?"

Our reply will always be, "Ask us in 20 years after these guys/gals have started their own families and careers."

Principle #3—Inside Person over the Outside Person

The words of Jesus are pointed and intensely inward-focused in Matthew 23:25–27: "Woe to you, scribes and Pharisees, hypocrites! For you clean the outside of the cup and plate, but inside they are full of greed and self-indulgence. You blind Pharisee! First clean the inside of the cup and the plate, that the outside also may be clean" (Matthew 23:26). In this account, Jesus goes on for two more verses stressing the importance of the inside person being in the right heart posture over the outward appearance.

I don't want to take this passage out of context and try to make it fit into a sports psychology analysis. However, the importance of the inner man appears to be more important to Jesus than the outside. We would say it is the same within athletics. The inside is just as important as the outside.

This is about the heart and the internal. The internal drives the external. Your heart, emotions, and thinking drive your behavior. We are always thinking about coaching the heart. We're not trying to be touchy-feely, per se; there's a practical aspect to that as well. However, we are spiritual, physical, mental, and emotional creatures. If all you do is coach—i.e., the physical—you're going to miss out on coaching the whole athlete. Regardless of the ability or how trained the athlete is, if the heart is wrong, if the attitude is wrong, if the athlete is in a bad emotional spot, his or her efforts will not translate into productivity.

Now, as mentioned earlier, the goal isn't productivity. However, at some point, we want our athletes to close the gap between their potential and their performance. The chance of closing that gap is linked significantly to where the head and heart are at on any particular day. Coaching the heart is one of the key foundations of this philosophy. In fact, most college and professional teams in any sport have a full-time mental/performance coach on their staff.

The term "coach" actually comes from the French word *coche*, a "large kind of four-wheeled, covered carriage."* In 1830, Oxford University had a slang term, "coach," for a tutor who "carries" a student through an exam. It is interesting that the word "coach" came from a student receiving help in their studies!

The positions of athletic trainer and coach have been around since the Greek games. However, the mental and internal side of coaching is fairly new within athletics. In 1974, Timothy Galloway wrote *The Inner Game of Tennis*. In this groundbreaking book, Galloway introduced the idea of a gap between sports coaching and personal development. Sports psychology was emphasized within athletics for the first time to this level and Galloway instantly became a leading innovator in the mental side of sports, his introduction to the inner game introduced a whole new mindset to athletes and coaches. Since then, from 1974 to 2024, we have seen sports become a multibillion-dollar industry. Thus, the need for coaching the internal and inner game is monumental.

Within the *Competing Biblically* philosophy, we emphasize the inner man as spiritual/mental. The ultimate goal is knowing who you are in Jesus and the redemption He has provided through the cross and resurrection. We are literally new creatures in Christ and play for an entirely different goal. We have the mind of Christ as we play—at least, that is the target. Talk about the mental and inner game! When you stop and think about the power we have as believers to actually believe we are filled with the Holy Spirit and play sports with His mind, His thinking, His way, it is an amazing, game-changing thought.

Here again, it is the internal driving the external. However, even as we realize and give credence to the importance of the inner game, we ask the question: *Do most coaches, including us, mostly coach the*

---

* *Online Etymology Dictionary.* https://www.etymonline.com/. Accessed May 20, 2025.

physical fundamentals and techniques? We believe the answer to that question is yes. We spend most of our time on the outward/physical part of the game. We would encourage coaches to consider coaching the inner game within their system because we understand the mind will shut down way before the body does. Special forces like the Army Rangers, Green Berets, and Navy Seals have demonstrated how far the body can go, which is much farther than we can see. Our mind and emotions, however, may not allow us to go there because they're blocked or unwilling. That's why the will is so important. We need everything aligned.

We're coaching the inside: the heart, invisible over the visible. It's a correlative thing. I can't see my heart; we're talking about the core being. I can't see my mind; I can't see my emotions. We're talking about the invisible *driving* what is visible. We are coaching up those things that are unseen, not to the neglect of competence, but along with it. This is not an either/or; it's a both. How's the athlete doing mentally? How's he doing emotionally? How's he doing spiritually? These are questions we ask within this philosophy, not just, "Is the athlete prepared technically?" Again, the mind, will, and emotions will shut down faster than the physical.

In Jesus' day, the Pharisees were all about the outward performance and Jesus was clear that we need to take care of the inside over the outside. I don't want to be called a white-washed tomb like He labelled them! Let's prepare our teams and coaches from the inside out.

Principle #4—The Weak over the Strong

This is a principle of God's heart for the poor and powerless. We also call them "the forgotten." On most teams, we're talking about athletes who don't naturally receive attention or credit like the starters and captains of the teams. The forgotten on a team are often going to be underclassmen who are younger. It may be people who don't play much or at all. It may be those who don't have as much talent, and whose roles aren't on the field, but they are very important.

Managers are very important in our programs, as are trainers. Obviously, they don't play in the game, but they're critical to what happens in the game, based on their job outside of the game. These are the people who need special emphasis and support because the game itself doesn't naturally give it to them.

We are often thinking about the athlete who doesn't play. *How is he or she feeling? What is he or she thinking?* In reality, any one of those athletes who don't play can end up being either an asset or a liability to the program. Worst-case scenario, if they're slandering us and their teammates behind the scenes or not supporting their teammates, it tears down the program. At some point, it's going to show up in the player's output and synergy because of the other principles we've talked about; unity and disunity, belief and unbelief, are all at stake.

The "Forgotten" may not necessarily be players; they could be the bus driver, the cafeteria worker serving the food, or the custodians. The people in these roles tend to be disrespected or not honored. I have seen people not pick up their trash in the cafeteria and dismissively say, "It's the custodian's job." But who doesn't want to be encouraged in their job?

So, in a culture of competing biblically, when you go to away games, you remember the forgotten ones. You say, "Thank you," to the bus driver; you look him or her in the eyes and you express gratitude for their contribution. You engage with the hotel desk workers. You say, "Thank you for working today."

When I visit a school and consult with them, I can discern the feel of the school when I go inside the cafeteria. Are different ethnic groups eating together or separately? Are athletes eating together or with the student body? Do athletes have their feet up like they rule the school? Can I tell who the athletes are? Generally, you can, unfortunately.

In the *Competing Biblically* philosophy, we would love our teams to be so embedded in the school that the school is one family. We do not want the culture to be about our team and then the school, but rather a culture where the team(s) and school are one big family.

Our vision is to have team members who are looking for the person who is eating by themselves. When our players walk into the cafeteria, they should at least have on their minds, not just, *Where are my buddies?* or *Where is it fun to sit?* Hopefully, it is on their radar to see anyone who looks alone, disenfranchised, or separate, and ask, "Can I sit with you?" That's a tremendous way to build an incredible and caring culture.

In junior high and high schools, and even small colleges, the student body is going to have a significant number of males who are into sports-related stuff. Sports tend to be intimidating to non-athletes, because athletes tend to have strong personalities—aggressive, and driven by ego. We want to teach our athletes, through sports, that it's about *others*: the disenfranchised, the poor and the powerless. Is the upperclassman looking to serve the underclassman? That's the opposite of the normal mentality, which is, *We're in charge now; we get to tell you what to do.* No, we encourage them, "You have given up your rights as an older team member and will now serve the younger!" What kind of amazing culture and team could that be?

Coach Frosty Westering, at Pacific Lutheran University in Tacoma, Washington, created a team where the younger teammates were embraced and embedded in the team from the first week. He set up a scenario he called "Breakaway" where the upperclassmen served the new players in the program and modeled servant leadership during the first week of football. Instead of the typical two-a-day during the first week, Frosty took the team to a camp on the Oregon Coast. At the camp, the freshmen would be served by the upperclassmen. The philosophy of servant leadership and the strong serving the weak played out with games and team bonding, in a fun atmosphere.

The team unity and synergy created by Frosty was legendary. This was part of that culture from the first week of practice. It obviously worked really well, as you can read for yourself in the memoir, *I Played for Frosty.* Many of the stories in that book are about players' memories of that first week in the program.

Does everyone in your program feel like they matter? The target we are aiming for is that everyone will feel like they matter, that they have value, regardless of performance, chronology, experience, or apparent maturity. The most mature are going to be the ones who go first and go further. The most mature are going to be the ones who die and give their life away.

In a healthy culture, the head coach is serving the assistants. The coaching staff are serving the players. The upperclassmen or more experienced players are serving the younger players. That's how you create culture, unity, synergy, and camaraderie. Protect the weak and young. Protect those who receive the least—the injured, those who don't play, those new to the system. They're not on the field, like managers and trainers. Serve those people well.

Principle #5—Interdependence over Independence

Merriam-Webster.com defines interdependence as "the state of being dependent upon one another: mutual dependence." The book *The Boys in the Boat*, now a motion picture, highlights the power of interdependence. Rowing, the subject of the book, demands teamwork and precise timing from each member. One member losing rhythm affects the whole crew.

Daniel James Brown, the author, describes the journey of teamwork during the 1936 Olympics, epitomizing interdependence:

> *"Perhaps the seeds of redemption lay not just in perseverance, hard work, and rugged individualism. Perhaps they lay in something more fundamental—the simple notion of everyone pitching in and pulling together. . . . They were now representatives of something much larger than themselves—a way of life, a shared set of values. Liberty was perhaps the most*

fundamental of those values. But the things that held them together—trust in each other, mutual respect, humility, fair play, watching out for one another—those were also part of what America meant to all of them."

The reward for the boys in the boat was a gold medal in front of Adolf Hitler and the world. However, it wasn't the "rugged individualism" that was the testimony to the world, but the "pitching in and pulling together" that would serve as symbolism for the eventual defeat of the Nazis and their cruel goal to conquer the then-known world. Although we as Americans love the idea of independence—and rightly so when it comes to our freedom—we recognize that our country has always been at its best when we unite as one and join forces in depending on each other. Interdependence is a crucial ingredient for *creating* independence and freedom. In that vein, the Church is also called to be in community and dependent on each other to walk in true freedom. Any great team will always possess the ingredient of depending on each other, especially during difficult times.

Each athlete will have their own individual personality. God made us with unique gifts and talents. However, while retaining our uniqueness, we, at the same time, want to submit our unique value to the whole. Our attitude needs to consider others more than ourselves. This was Paul's attitude as he said (and this is my paraphrase), "I want to be all things to all men so that if at all possible, I can save some. If I like meat and it offends you, I'll never eat meat again in front of you." (See 1 Corinthians 8:12-13.) This is the heart of beginning to understand what's best for the team and not what's best for me; if it's best for the team, that's what I want.

And that's the philosophy we're trying to create: *I'm going to take my independence and I'm going to submit it and become interdependent, which means I receive the benefits and the responsibilities.* You don't simply receive benefits. When you receive increased benefits, you have increased responsibilities. We want to teach this within the context of sport.

Our desire is for our athletes to learn to be great husbands, fathers, workers, friends, mothers, and wives. This is what we're trying to create. We do it through sport as we teach these values to our teams. Every strong team and organization will have a strong foundation of interdependence within its structure. Never underestimate the power of Acts 2:46–47: "Every day they continued to meet together in the temple courts. They broke bread in their homes and ate together with glad and sincere hearts, praising God and enjoying the favor of all the people. And the Lord added to their number daily those who were being saved." The early Church depended on each other and our hope is that same spirit will be displayed on our teams.

Principle #6–Process over Results

Scotty Kessler was asked, "What is process over results to you?". I will paraphrase his thoughts on this important topic. He always encourages his teams to *focus* on the process over results. Outcomes are just byproducts, and our job is to practice, prepare, and perform according to God's word. Preparation is key, but victory or defeat rests in the Lord. We aim for faithfulness and perseverance, not records or awards. The most important action is always the next one, not the current score. Strive for perfection in technique and fundamentals, not in the scoreboard.

John Wooden said, "It is the little details that are vital. Little things make big things happen."

I believe Coach Wooden is talking about the process over results in that quote. When you take care of the little details and treat them as vital, I believe the results will take care of themselves. Likewise, if you don't take care of the little details, the results you don't want will still take care of themselves.

Nick Saban, the former coach of the Alabama Crimson Tide, told his teams, "Don't think about winning the SEC championship. Don't think about winning the national championship. Think about what you need to do in this drill, on this play, in this moment. That's the process: let's think about what we can do today, the task at hand."

Coach Saban also has some excellent teaching on this subject of process. He taught his teams to do the following:

- Focus on the present. Focus on what you can do today, rather than worrying about the future.
- Embrace process thinking. Focus on how things are done, rather than just the outcome.

Frosty called this the Success Road as opposed to the Road to Success. It seems like these great coaches figured it out in convincing their teams not to get caught up in the result or scoreboard. True Success will come when you take care of the process. Commit to the process.

My friend coaches a Little League team. He asked me to speak to his team because they had had a rough week in the win-loss column. They informed me that they had gone 1–3 and were frustrated in their play. However, while I watched them practice and observed the drills they were participating in, I could see that they were not taking care of the little details in their fundamentals. A few guys were swinging the bat and pulling their head off the ball; kids pitching in the bullpen were not concentrating on their mechanics. I could tell by observation that they were definitely not taking care of the details.

Thus, I began my talk to them about process over results. I told them that they seemed like they were more concerned about the scoreboard and the outcome than they were about taking care of what they could control like their own efforts, preparation, and attitude at practice. I told them about our saying, inherited from Frosty, "They come to beat us, we come to be us." In this philosophy of *Competing Biblically*, we are not concerned about who we play or what the results will be on the scoreboard. The biggest concern should be taking care of the process and what we can control, which, in this case, was improving on the fundamentals of the game of baseball at practice.

Discussion Questions

1. Team over Individual: In what ways can a coach or athlete demonstrate putting the team before their own individual needs, especially in high-pressure situations? How does this principle align with Jesus' example of humility and sacrifice?

2. Inside Person over Outside Person: How can coaches intentionally focus on the inner development of their athletes (spiritually, mentally, emotionally) while also working on physical and technical skills? What are some practical ways to assess and nurture the "inner game" of an athlete?

3. Principle #4 emphasizes serving those who are often overlooked or forgotten. How can we as coaches or team members create an environment where the "forgotten" players and staff feel valued and supported, even if they don't directly contribute to the game's outcome?

4. Interdependence, as described in Principle #5, stresses the importance of teamwork and mutual reliance. How can we cultivate a mindset where athletes submit their individual strengths to serve the collective good of the team, especially in competitive environments?

5. Principle #6 encourages a focus on the process rather than the results. How can we help athletes shift their mindset from focusing on winning to valuing the development of skills, character, and team cohesion? What strategies can we use to keep them motivated even when the results are not immediately favorable?

As a Coach—take care of what you can take care of. Are you practicing excellence in your coaching? Is your practice plan detailed? What is your scope and sequence of your coaching during a season? Are you a student of your particular sport with the idea of developing your athletes to maximize their potential? Simply put, are you a "Coaching Excellence Coach?" From a spiritual aspect, are you praying over your team and coaches? It's not our job to see the results of prayer, although it is great to see God operate and move in lives. At the end of the day, it is our job to pray and intercede for the people/team under our care. I feel convicted about this even as I write. Am I taking care of the process of prayer for the organization I am working with? There is therefore no condemnation. If you haven't been interceding for your team, teammates, family . . . Repent, and begin praying.

As an Athlete—are you taking care of the process? How is your attitude, preparation, and effort? We all love great results as athletes, but are you more concerned about the daily drill and daily process? Feel the joy and freedom of the process.

As a Parent—are you taking care of the process of supporting your child? Are you supporting the coaches? Are you looking to build relationships with other parents in seeing them come into the Kingdom? Are you honoring the officials—or "letting them have it" from the stands? Are you enjoying the process of seeing your kids play and participate in sports? Trust me, it goes by really fast and your days at the field or gym are suddenly gone as your kids grow up. These are great days! Enjoy them and enjoy the process.

CHAPTER 5

PLAY THE S.U.B.S.
(THE 4 PILLARS OF COMPETING BIBLICALLY)

"Unless the Lord builds the house, those who build it labor in vain."
—Psalm 127:1

There is a double meaning with the word "pillar." In building terms, it means a tall, vertical structure of stone, wood, or metal, used as a support for a building. It can also be defined as a person or thing regarded as reliably providing support for something.

In the context of *Competing Biblically*, the four pillars represent both meanings of the word. We believe the pillars help support the framework of the philosophy. We also believe that coaches and athletes will become pillars for their teams and communities as they apply the principles of the Word of God to their coaching, playing, and leading. The Lord is the builder of this house we call *Competing Biblically*. We believe when we trust in Him and His process of building, then we can become the pillars we are called to be as leaders in our sphere of influence.

The Four Pillars of Competing Biblically

The "S.U.B.S" are Selflessness versus Selfishness, Unity versus Disunity, Belief versus Unbelief, and Submissiveness versus Unsubmissiveness:

Concept	Positive	Negative
S.U.B.S	Selflessness	Selfishness
	Unity	Disunity
	Belief	Unbelief
	Submissiveness	Unsubmissiveness

1. SelfLESSness vs. Selfishness

"Unless a seed falls to the ground and dies, it cannot bear fruit."
John 12:24

Philippians 2:3–4 has been a convicting scripture for me over the years: "Do nothing out of selfish ambition or vain conceit. Rather, in humility value others above yourselves, not looking to your own interests but each of you to the interests of others." I know I had selfish ambition episodes in my playing days and coaching days. I never considered myself an egomaniac, but I do remember times when I was upset I went 0-for-4 at the plate, even though we won the game. As Scotty Kessler says, "If you cut us open and look inside, you will find selfishness in all of us."

This is the conundrum. We really want to glorify God in all we do, but the sin nature is so strong in the area of athletics. It is a real-life battle that will continue until we go on to Heaven. Our will versus His will is played out daily on this planet. The athletic field is the great laboratory to flush out our flesh. At the end of the day, we are to follow the path Jesus laid out for us in Philippians 2:7–8, ". . . rather, he made himself nothing by taking the very nature of a servant, being made in human likeness. And being found in appearance as a man, he humbled himself by becoming obedient to death-even death on a cross!" Jesus literally left the splendor of heaven to come to Planet Earth and become the epitome of servant leadership.

We will always teach to give it our absolute best shot in our attitude, preparation, and effort. However, at the end of the day, we believe in competing and living a selfless life. On the other side of the coin is selfishness. Selfishness is about me and I. This is like holiness and unholiness. One is a good thing that bears good fruit, the other is a bad thing that bears bad fruit.

Selfishness will kill a team faster than anything. A selfish head coach, if he thinks it's about him, will never take responsibility for anything. He'll blame his coaches; he'll blame his players. There is nothing worse than a guy who says, "Yeah, I made a mistake, but so did you." He's not repentant. That is not a healthy place to live. A healthy environment is, "God have mercy on me, for I am a sinner!" If I'm a head coach and it hasn't gone well, I'd better realize, *I didn't do a good job.* I either allowed it or caused it to happen. Something needs to be fixed and it's my responsibility because it is my team. I'm not saying the assistants and players don't have some responsibility. But blaming is out of the question when somebody takes full responsibility.

Selfish coaches and players, on the other hand, will never take responsibility. A selfish coach won't do that if he's afraid of his reputation. He won't do that if he thinks people won't respect him if he says, "It's my fault, I'm sorry, please forgive me." But if he doesn't do that, he's not going to have a healthy climate.

That doesn't mean he won't win. If he's got a lot of talent, he can still win, even if the climate is horrific. I've been part of teams that had horrific climates; they just had a ton of talent. I've been a part of teams that had no talent but great climates. I promise you, I'd rather be on a team with a fantastic climate than a team that wins with a selfish coach and players! You may have a ring, you may have a trophy, you may have memories, but they're not going to be good.

This is why it's so important to pound away consistently at the To-By-For philosophy, praying for the power of the Holy Spirit to fill us and enable us to compete according TO His word, BY His power, and FOR His glory.

Another great point to make about selflessness is what Frosty Westering used to call "Flush it." When a mistake was made during a game, Frosty would yell, "Flush it!" That meant forget about it. Move on to the next play. Not to move on would actually be a case of selfishness, indicating that as a player you were more concerned about your mistake than moving on for the sake of the team.

Selfishness, in this case, blocks your potential to perform. If you carry your negative attitude into the next play, that next play may be compromised. It is a spiritual principle as well. You made a mistake: confess your sin, accept forgiveness, and live free. Move on. We must engage in the battle without wasting time on self-despair.

Follow biblical principles for guidance, knowing that failure is part of the process. With failure comes forgiveness through confession and repentance. Be selfless and remember that being part of a team means prioritizing *us* over yourself.

2. Unity vs. Disunity

Unity and disunity both have significant impacts. Jesus highlighted that a little leaven could affect the entire dough (see Galatians 5:9, ESV). Leaven, when added to bread, causes it to rise and spread.

An Old Testament story recounts Achan's transgression. After Israel defeated a foreign enemy, Ai, in battle, God instructed the Israelites to destroy all the enemy's goods and not keep anything for themselves. However, Achan took some spoils of war, hid them in his tent, and buried them. When Israel engaged in another battle, they were unexpectedly defeated. Joshua, their leader, questioned God about the defeat, reminding Him of His promise of victory (see Joshua 7).

God informed Joshua that there was sin within the camp because someone had taken forbidden spoils and hidden them; that disobedience led to their defeat. This story illustrates the principle of leadership and collective responsibility.

Joshua faced judgment due to one person's disobedience among two million. This underscores the importance of accountability in leadership. Job also prayed for his children's protection and sought forgiveness for any actions of theirs that might have offended God.

Each individual is responsible for their own actions. However, the concept of corporate responsibility is also significant. This principle is observed in biblical texts such as Ezra, Nehemiah, and Daniel, where these leaders sought forgiveness on behalf of the people. Although they had not sinned personally, they requested forgiveness for the sins of Israel: "And the Israelites separated themselves from all foreigners and stood and confessed their sins and the iniquities of their fathers" (Nehemiah 9:2). These leaders recognized the need for accountability within leadership roles.

One cannot simply state, "I didn't do it." Instead, there is a collective responsibility: "We did it." If a member of a team makes an error, the entire team is impacted by that individual's decision. Whether it be in the dormitory or the city, the actions of one team member affect the whole team. This illustrates both the advantages and disadvantages of teamwork. No team member operates in isolation; corporate responsibility is essential.

As a former head coach, I emphasized the importance of being part of a team. I would remind players that their conduct in the dorms affected everyone else because we are all associated with one another. Some players might believe that they have more freedom once the season ends. However, I would clarify that they remained part of the team throughout the year. Even though we were not playing year-round, they were still representatives of our team. While their choice of religious worship remained personal, their behavior on campus and in town must align with the values of our football program and represent our school positively.

Our team members must follow our vision and leadership. As John Wooden said, "When you choose to be part of a team, you cease to exist as an individual." Unity is crucial. In the Bible, Achan's wrongdoing led to the camp losing its battle against Ai, illustrating the importance of unity and fearing God.

This principle shows that one person's actions can affect the whole group. Therefore, unity and respect are essential. I told my staff, "Respect and honor me not for my sake but for the team's unity. Any disunity or disrespect will diminish our power and incur discipline." We need to maintain unity and fear God to ensure our success.

These are core convictions to drive the culture that creates the climate that results in maximizing performance personally and corporately, and that glorifies God. He is not interested in championship rings. He doesn't need you to win a title so you can position yourself to testify because the world appreciates somebody who wins more than they don't. He doesn't need help glorifying Himself. He'd love us to *enhance* His glory by choice and decision. But He doesn't want to use inappropriate, non-biblical, non-Holy Spirit-driven means to that end. He's got more than enough glory for Himself by Himself! He's simply allowing us to participate in the process.

3. Belief vs. Unbelief

We know the power of belief. We know that someone can translate from hell to heaven by his confession. Somebody can go to eternity for billions of years, with God or separated from Him, based on belief on the name of Lord Jesus.

We understand from the book of James that demons believe and shudder. Belief isn't just knowing something but being committed in your heart to something or someone. In the early days of Jesus' ministry,

He invited His disciples to follow Him. Following Jesus meant a life of obedience to His teachings and the example of His life. Even today, the sign of a believer is that they obey, not that they raise their hand in a church service. First John 2:3–4 says, "We know we have come to know Him if we keep His commands." Whoever says they know Him, "but does not do as He commands is a liar and the truth is not in him."

The sign of a believer is not his confession; the sign is his or her obedience and willingness. For us, it is not just a casual, "Yeah, I believe in this philosophy," but a commitment that we give our lives to it and its biblical foundation.

I have had to hire coaches over the years, and when I interviewed them in the vetting process, they said they believed in the *Competing Biblically* philosophy. I believe that they believed they believed. However, as soon as we got onto the grass and adversity hit—either a bad call or play—it fractured their belief because there wasn't an actual buy-in. Their confession was loud, and they raised their hand to show that they believed in the biblical approach to coaching. However, they did not walk out the confession with the keeping of coaching "according TO His Word."

There is the legendary story about the Spanish explorer, Cortez, arriving in the New World in 1519 and facing some rebellion from his troops, who wanted to return to Spain. As the troops were marching inland, they looked back and saw that their boats were on fire. Cortez had burned the boats. He burned their chance to go back. By his leadership he forced them to buy in; there was no turning back. Two years later, he succeeded in his complete conquest of the Aztec Empire.

That is how this philosophy has to be approached, in our opinion. You either buy in for the whole enchilada or it's not going to work. You can't "kind of" follow Jesus. When you do that, it won't work. Some people will try to do it by their own power, or their own glory. But it only works if you die to yourself. It only works if it's *His* power, *His* glory, *His* Word. For it to work the way it was designed to work, it's all or nothing. For this philosophy to fly, you have to put to death yourself, the scoreboard, and your desire to beat or dominate people. Those goals will tease you and compromise you from the foundational core belief that this is To-By-For. This is our conviction.

Early on, I was one of the coaches who used this philosophy of life like a buffet table and chose what I wanted. I wanted some of the ideas but still thought I needed a target, like winning the state championship. Now, I would contend that you don't have to say that. You may *think* you have to say that because the world says that. You may think that is a great motivator. But I promise you: it's not. I've coached a long time and all I can say is when your goal is the league championship, and you lose the game that would enable you to make that championship, and you have five games left, it changes your motivation. It changes your team's motivation. They'd have to be incredibly mature to lose their chance of achieving their goal and stay motivated when their goal is a faulty goal.

When you have a goal that's too low, that's a problem. When you have a goal that's too high that's a problem. According to Wes Neal, in *The Handbook,* these goals, when they are not biblically driven goals, are difficult for sustainability. It doesn't mean they're sin; they're just problematic because they're going to demotivate you and your team. Look how hard teams play when they're behind by a ton, when they lose the chance to win the game, or when they are in early-season practice versus the practice before the game. There is a different feel for most teams and coaches. If your goal is just to get through practice, you are not going to maximize your ability. If your goal is to get through practice just to be able to play in the game, you're not going to maximize your preparation, even if you're operating from a worldly perspective. That type of motivation will compromise your preparation, and if your preparation is compromised, your productivity is compromised.

Belief versus unbelief is critical. When you have a team that believes, you have a chance to maximize ability. Where there is unbelief, it is a crack in your pillar and the collapse of your house is inevitable. Unbelief in your head coach, if you're an assistant, compromises your productivity. Unbelief in each other compromises your experience as coaches, which compromises the players. Unbelief of the players in the coaches causes a rift in the locker room—people get fired because they've lost their team. That means the team has lost buy-in with the coach or the organization. Do you see where unbelief leads?

Have you ever played or coached a team that had one player who was a bad apple? Sometimes those players are called "cancers" on the team. The player speaks ill of his teammates, is selfish, and talks badly about the coaches behind the scenes. That one player can change the entire culture and do damage to a locker room and clubhouse. That player has an unbelief in the program.

For this reason, when we consult with coaches, we recommend they hire assistants who buy into the vision completely. It matters less about their experience in coaching, than that they believe in the coach and his/her vision. Their job is to implement the vision.

Will some of the assistants have a different vision? Sure, they will; they're different people with different styles. If some of them were the head coach, they would do it differently. I've said to my own assistants, "I know you would do it differently." I'd be shocked if anybody said, "Sure, Coach; everything you do is the way it should be done!" When somebody wouldn't do everything the same way, that's not rebellion. That's just a human living with his own convictions. The thing is, *Am I willing to die to myself, die to my vision, and submit to the leader?* There is an authority-submission dynamic that allows me to give my whole self to something that would not necessarily be my flavor. That is real life. We are not talking about blind obedience. We are talking about submitting our will to the leader or team.

Belief over unbelief has to be one of the pillars supporting the program being built. The great news is that we can do this BY the power of the Holy Spirit. We don't have to muster up our own efforts to see this accomplished. We can pray, "Jesus, I believe in You and Your ways. I want to know You and trust in You: I want to follow You and obey Your commands in leading this team. Lead through me and help me to be a pillar of belief for the sake of Your Kingdom and Your glory." Amen!

4. Submissiveness vs. Unsubmissiveness

I love the story of Coach John Wooden's rule of no facial hair for his team. Bill Walton was the star center and showed up to practice with a beard after a 10-day layoff. Coach Wooden asked him if he had forgotten the rule. Bill Walton informed the coach that he felt it was his right to have the beard and he should be allowed to keep it. Coach Wooden asked him if he really believed that. Bill informed Coach that he really believed it strongly. Coach Wooden then told him how much he respected individuals that stood up for what they believed in. He then went on to tell him how much the team was going to miss him. Bill Walton immediately went into the locker room and shaved the beard off.

When we talk about submission versus lack of submission, we realize that it may trigger a lot of emotion in some readers. There are some of us who have backgrounds and experiences where authority figures in our lives lorded their authority over us, or even used it to abuse us. That's not the kind of authority we're talking about. In this context, we are talking about healthy relationships. We are not talking about submitting to authority figures that caused you to do something illegal or unbiblical. We are not talking about blind obedience; we're talking about eyes-open obedience. In this context, we are talking about order and disorder. We are talking about a John Wooden to Bill Walton dialogue, about a team rule and philosophy.

God is a God of order. What order is to us and what order is to God may be two different things. In general, there needs to be order in an organization. Think about what you want as a parent of your kids. Think about what you want as an employer of your employees, and what would be acceptable positions for employees following their employers. When we talk about submission and lack of submission, we're talking about doing what we're asked to do by those who have been placed in positions of authority over us.

The 10 Commandments talk about children honoring and obeying their parents. This commandment is the fourth commandment and doesn't have the caveat, "If you feel like it, then obey your parents." It simply says to obey them so things will go well for you.

When I was a kid, I didn't always hold to that philosophy and disobeyed and dishonored my parents on occasion. Most of the time, those acts of disobedience were times I now regret. I paid the price for my disobedience. As I became a parent and had my kids repeat some of my behavior, I felt the sting of disobedient kids. It is true that you reap what you sow. I didn't feel bad just because of their disobedience, but I knew the pain and/or destruction that awaited their choice of not following my instructions. This is what we're trying to teach the people we are coaching. Whether they're five or 25, we're trying to teach them a principle: *Your job is to do your job and my job is to do my job. I coach; you play. Don't mix up the jobs. The referee is the ref. You are not the ref. Don't mix up the jobs.*

We always teach various roles at an athletic contest. There are the players, the coaches, the officials, and the fans. Choose one role and do that really well. If you are a player, just play the game. You don't have to stress out about the calls; simply submit yourself to the officials and let them do their job. If you are a parent/fan, submit yourself to the coaches and officials, and enjoy the game. That means my job as a player is to say, "Not my will, but yours be done, Coach." That means my job an assistant coach is to say, "Not my will, but yours be done, head coach." Once again, that doesn't mean the assistants don't have a different conviction. They just choose to submit their conviction to the will of God, and who He has placed in authority, and trust God with it.

My job is to help the head coach reach his goal. My job as a player is to help the program reach its goals. My job as an employee is to help the employer reach their goal. It's not my board game. I work for them and with them. We both work together, but we understand order and we understand authority. If you don't understand team and organizational order, you will have a breakdown of the team. Do you want to be in a society where people don't stop at stoplights and don't obey any laws? Do you want to be in a basketball game where there are no fouls and no out of bounds? Is that going to be an enjoyable experience for everyone? Without order and boundaries, you will not enjoy the experience.

Competing biblically has the Garden of Gethsemane mantra of "not my will, but Yours be done." We believe the principle of dying to self ends up gaining more life and impact. These are all things Jesus told us on the front end. Unfortunately, it took us time to buy into that, and many of us are still arriving to the Garden of Gethsemane, learning to lay down our own rights and agendas.

Discussion Questions

1. Selflessness vs. Selfishness: How does the concept of selflessness in competition challenge your natural instincts as an athlete or coach? Can you think of a time when embracing selflessness enhanced your team's performance or culture?

2. Unity vs. Disunity: How can the actions of one team member, as illustrated in the biblical story of Achan, impact the unity of a whole team or organization? What are some practical ways to foster unity in a team setting?

3. Belief vs. Unbelief: How does the principle of belief in the vision or philosophy of a coach impact team performance? Have you ever been part of a team where belief or unbelief significantly influenced the culture or results?

4. Submissiveness vs. Unsubmissiveness: What role does submission to leadership play in creating a healthy team environment? How can coaches encourage submission to authority without creating an atmosphere of blind obedience?

SECTION 3

The TO-BY-FOR Philosophy

CHAPTER 6

THE 4 BLESSINGS OF COMPETING BIBLICALLY
THE BRANCHES

"And I will make you a great nation, and I will
bless you and make your name great,
so that you will be a blessing."
—Genesis 12:2 (ESV)

"But to those who are listening I say: Love your ene-
mies. Do good to those who hate you. BLESS those
who curse you. Pray for those who mistreat you."
—Luke 6:27–28 (NIV)

Blessing by definition, is an undeserved gift, or grace. Because
grace is a gift freely given not earned, it makes little sense. It's
upside down. When we really begin to grasp that the blessing
God offers in Jesus Christ is completely undeserved, we begin
to freely give it away to others in the midst of competition,
even when it's not deserved, or we get nothing in return."
—Brian Peterson—Co-Founder—Reality Sports

The *Competing Biblically* philosophy operates within four channels of blessing:

1. Bless your teammates/leaders
2. Bless the opponent
3. Bless the officials
4. Bless the forgotten

We want to emphasize the idea that these Four Components of Blessing are essential; the philosophy depends on creating a culture of blessing. This is a matter of heart condition. The driving force is Genesis 12, where it talks about Abraham's conversation with God, the Abrahamic Blessing.

There are a number of blessings in the first five books of the Old Testament. The Abrahamic Blessing can be distilled down to, "I'm blessing you so that you may be a blessing to others." We were not blessed by the Lord merely for our own personal benefit, but so that all families on Earth may be blessed through us. (Genesis 12:1–3, NLV) In modern terminology, it's similar to the concept of "paying it forward"—"I'm going to fill you, so that you empty yourself, so that I can fill you, so that you empty yourself." In this way, we want to create a culture of blessing. We're interested in blessing the opponent, the referees, the restaurant workers, the hotel workers, the fans—anybody in the outer circle.

We certainly want to bless the inner circle, the teammates and coaches. The inner circle in your family would be your siblings and parents. (You can read more about developing your inner and outer circles in Chapter 11). But we also want to bless anybody who's associated, anybody with whom we have contact in any way, shape, or form. This is "who we are, not what we do." We are blessers. God created us to be blessers. He blessed us so that we would bless others. He gave it to us so that we would give ourselves away.

Being filled is a continuous process of being filled and refilled (see Ephesians 5:13). It's like the metaphor we use in our discipleship class, about how the Jordan River, in the Holy Land, runs into the Sea of Galilee. It then runs out of the Sea of Galilee and into the Dead Sea. This is the reason why the Sea of Galilee is alive; the Jordan River runs in and runs out, which keeps it fresh and alive. The reason why the Dead Sea is dead, even though the Jordan River runs into it, is because nothing comes out. If you don't bless, though you've been blessed, you lose your blessing; you become dead—not literally, not physiologically, but you're dead in terms of your spiritual impact. You're dead in terms of your reproductive capacity and then multiplication is out the window.

We are blessed—the Jordan River flows into us—and we are a blessing, which keeps us alive. What others do with their blessing is between them and their Maker. Our job is to do our job. God's job is to do God's job. People's response to that is between them and the Lord.

A "culture of blessing," like we see described in Genesis 12, is at the core of the *Competing Biblically* philosophy because it's a defining question to think about philosophically as a staff or family. Are we a blessing to everyone within our sphere of influence? Do we need to be more conscious of blessing others? How did we bless others today?

An encouraging word is a blessing. A put up (as opposed to a "put down") is a blessing. Cleaning the locker room is a blessing. Making a room or a better situation than it was before we arrived is a blessing. These are all manifestations of blessings that are part of the culture. We're teaching people how to serve others for their best to the glory of God according **TO** the Word of God, **BY** His power, and **FOR** His Glory. This is the culture we're trying to create.

The FOOT Principle

Here we want to break down in sequence the Four Blessings. As stated earlier in this book, we want to create easy ways to memorize the foundations and precepts we believe in. My friend and co-founder at Reality Sports, Brian Peterson, flipped the acronym for the Four Blessings to spell the word F.O.O.T. These four components of a blessing are to bless the:

F orgotten

O fficials

O pponents

T eammates

As you can see, when you flip it to F.O.O.T., it has a "serve first" mentality. Of course, we know the story of Jesus washing the feet of His disciples. We are calling upon our athletes and coaches to "wash feet" like Jesus did.

It is fascinating to look at that passage in John 13 where Jesus displays true servant leadership in the foot-washing ceremony. Recently, I read the first part of John 13 again and saw something I had never seen before. In John 13:3–4, it says, "Jesus, knowing that the Father had given all things into his hands, and that he had come from God and was going back to God, rose from supper. He laid aside his outer garments, and taking a towel, tied it around his waist" (ESV). It goes on to talk about Jesus washing the disciples' feet, but I caught something in verse 3 that struck my heart. In verse 3, Jesus knows that the Father has given all things into His hands. Jesus knows He is receiving all glory and honor, yet at this moment, He doesn't gloat or sit in pride in His glory but does one of the humblest acts of that particular culture, He washes feet.

This is the King of Kings and Lord of Lords humbling Himself and demonstrating what sacrifice and love look like in servanthood. This is just the beginning of His display of sacrifice as the cross awaits Him in the next 24 hours. This act of blessing His disciples goes beyond our human comprehension. In the height of knowing your glory, wash feet.

The demonstration Jesus gave at that time is that we are called to do the same thing. We are called to be servant warriors and fulfill the FOOT blessings. He gave us His Holy Spirit to enable us to pull this off. There is no way we can do this on our own. Every human being will always veer toward pride when glory comes our way; it is our "nature."

But, we possess His nature now as we have been transformed by the blood of Christ. We are filled by the same Spirit who raised Jesus from the grave, living in us (See Romans 8:11). SO, we can walk in humility and we CAN, by the grace of God, wash feet. Let's keep going with our FOOT discipleship process!

1. **Bless the Forgotten**

   As players and coaches, we are called to follow Christ's example of seeing and serving those who are often overlooked. In Mark 10:46, Jesus encounters Bartimaeus, a blind man sitting by the roadside, whom many tried to silence. Yet Jesus stopped, listened, and blessed him with healing. This was an era in history where there were no government agencies helping the poor and the powerless. Individuals with sickness, blindness, and poverty were mostly on their own with no help but to beg for mercy. Jesus was on His way to Jerusalem to do "ministry." He was on a mission with purpose.

   However, Jesus gives us an example that the road to ministry WAS the ministry. While others were telling Bartimaeus to be quiet, Jesus stopped his trip for a moment to heal Bartimaeus. How are we "on our way" to the big game or practice? Do we acknowledge the poor and powerless/forgotten people in our path? We must open our eyes to the "Bartimaeuses" around us—such as bus drivers, bench players, the chain gang on the sidelines of a football game, and game clock managers. These individuals may not always be in the spotlight, but they play a vital role in the game. By showing them kindness, offering a word of gratitude, or praying for their needs, we reflect the love of Christ and remind them they are seen and valued.

   You are on a mission in your sport as a coach, athlete, parent, or fan. Who are the poor and powerless/forgotten in your path? Another question is: who are the forgotten in your everyday life outside the field of play? What about your siblings? Parents? Widows, Orphans, the fatherless? How about those sitting by themselves in the cafeteria? The kids who look like they don't have many friends?

We pray that coaches take the time to teach their athletes to have a heart for the forgotten on their campus. We pray that coaches, athletes, and parents realize that sin has blinded the minds of unbelievers. While Bartimaeus was physically blind, there are people around us every day who are spiritually blind. We have the light of Christ within us to shine brightly. The power of the Word of God is in our hearts and when we are bold enough to display that light with our play and coaching, darkness must flee at the sound of Jesus' name and the power of the gospel. (See James 4:7.) Let's keep our spiritual antennae up to be aware of the Forgotten.

2. Bless the Officials

Blessing the officials begins with controlling what we can control—our attitude, preparation, and effort. Proverbs 21:31 reminds us, "The horse is made ready for the day of battle, but the victory belongs to the Lord." We prepare diligently and give our best, trusting God with the outcome. This means we don't waste energy arguing over bad calls or showing poor body language when things don't go our way. Instead, we choose respect and self-discipline, knowing our response reflects our faith. Captains can set the tone by introducing themselves to the referees before the game and thanking them afterward. A simple "thank you" or handshake shows appreciation for their role in keeping the game fair and orderly, and it blesses them in ways we may never fully see. There are certain things we have no control over in a competition.

Many times, we cannot control injuries. We physically train to the best of our ability, but athletes get injured. We cannot control the weather. At some level, we can't control the outcome/results. I can hit a line drive in baseball, but possibly right at the shortstop for an out. I can only take care of what I can control.

One thing for certain is that I cannot control the officials' calls. I understand what it is like to become bent out of shape during a contest when it feels like all the calls are going against you. I know what it is like to try to "work the officials" to get calls to go your way. I was coaching in a game early in my career when Scotty Kessler was in attendance. I was "working the umpire" a little bit by asking the catcher where the pitch was located after the umpire called a borderline pitch a ball. I went on to say something like this, "Hey, where was that pitch?" (Talking to my catcher, of course.) And I abruptly said quickly, "That ball's not down; come on, now." It was a subtle approach to the umpire that he needed to get the strike zone correct and give us that "borderline" strike call.

This type of language is common in the baseball world and would not appear to be "too disrespectful" but just part of the game. The umpire didn't even acknowledge me, as he knew what I was doing. Now, after the game, Kess had a different idea about how my approach to the umpire was, in the sense of competing biblically. Kess simply asked me about the situation: what was I attempting in that moment?

I filled him in on the baseball ethics and tradition of baseball allowing for the head coach to chirp from the dugout on close calls. The chirping is allowed to a point, but once that line is crossed with a continuing barrage from the coach, most umpires will give a warning for the coach to "knock it off." I had not crossed the line in this situation, at least according to the traditional baseball world.

However, Kess gave his opinion in the form of a question. He asked me, "What if it's God's will that the other team wins that at bat?" The question threw me a little bit because I had not really thought about it that way. I suppose I knew that God knew the outcome of the game and whether or not He even cared about who won or lost wasn't on my radar. I had never prayed about God's will being done for the outcome of a game, much less worried about whether a ball or strike was called by the umpire. I just knew I was doing all I could to get the calls to go "our way" and win the game.

When I stopped to think (and pray) about my "traditional and accepted" behavior as the head coach, I personally felt convicted. I was part of a tradition that actually dishonors (the opposite of honor and bless) officials. But just because something has been done for a long time doesn't make it right.

Now, to be clear, I think it is okay and within the coaches' duty and responsibility to talk respectfully to officials about calls missed or questionable calls within the rules. I think we know what those situations are. I know that we all know when the line is crossed and it is becoming unbiblical. For some reason, in our culture, we have accepted the falsehood that it is okay to berate officials from the field as an athlete, from the bench as a coach, and from the stands as a parent or fan. Some of the worst fans I have heard have been at games when Christian schools are playing each other.

God, have mercy on us in those situations, like the scene of cursing officials in the gym and then walking across the parking lot or street to attend the church affiliated with the high school. As the book of James says, "Out of the mouth come praise and cursing. My brothers and sisters, this should not be" (James 3:10).

3. Bless Your Opponents

The opponent in our culture has been associated with words like Rival, Foe, and Enemy. The enemy or opponent is Jesus' day was the Roman Empire. Jesus told His disciples to "love their enemies." What!? How and why would we ever do that?

Under Armour had a famous slogan a few years ago: "Not in our house!" Of course, this was referring to home-field advantage and the idea that it is a place we will protect at all costs. "This is our home turf and someone else is coming in here to take away from us?" No way!

In my days as a player, I had a coach who used to give a pre-game speech about how the opponent was coming into "our house" to take away our hopes and dreams. Everything we had worked for up to that moment was being threatened by these villains/opponents. I remember feeling kind of pumped up about the speech, but I had friends on the other team and knew they were not really trying to destroy my goals and dreams in life. They just wanted to beat me in football or baseball and then laugh and brag about it later. Even at a higher level of competition, most of us were having fun competing against each other.

I do realize there are some legitimate "rivalry games" out there and some teams really don't like each other. However, it doesn't matter what tradition or culture says about "it's okay to hate someone else." If it doesn't line up with the Word, then it is off the table. I believe you can play with ferocity, and I would even say more ferocity, following the principle of competing "with all your heart," than you can with rivalry hate. So, when we say "bless the opponent" it means *all the time*. We don't get to say, "Yes, I agree with that . . . until we play Michigan (if you are from Ohio State)." ☺

How do we bless our opponents? The key to blessing your opponents can be found in Jesus' teaching in Luke 6:27–28: "Love your enemies, do good to those who hate you, bless those who curse you, pray for those who mistreat you." We like to break that down to four steps: Love—Do good—Bless—Pray.

Loving your opponents means respecting the game by giving your best effort—your effort honors their hard work too.

Doing good might look like offering a hand to help them up after a play, even if they see you as an enemy. If they curse or taunt you, bless them with a kind word like "great hit" or "good play." And no matter how they treat you, pray for them. Asking God to guide and bless them transforms your heart and honors Christ. The ultimate reason why we "bless our opponent" is because Jesus blessed us. In Romans 5:8 it says, "But God demonstrates his own love for us in this: while we were still sinners, Christ died for us."

4. **Bless Your Teammates and Coaches/Leaders**

Teammates and coaches are your inner circle—the people you spend the most time with. Outside of sports, this includes siblings, parents, and immediate family. Sometimes, those closest to you are the hardest to bless. In sports, your inner circle is your teammates. *We might ask: How do I bless my teammates? Why is it challenging to bless them?* There is pride, selfishness, sin, and various personalities on a team. In our minds, our teammates may not deserve to be loved or blessed. Why then must we still bless them? It is called "grace"—undeserved blessing. A blessing isn't deserved. We don't earn blessings. We give and receive blessings.

How do we achieve a blessing culture? We can look to Mark 12:31 for insight on how we might bless our teammates—loving our neighbors as ourselves. When we love each other well, the whole world will know we are Jesus' disciples. This love shows up in consistent encouragement: give great verbal "put-ups" throughout the game and after. Celebrate each other's efforts and lift each other up when mistakes happen.

You know you are on a special team when you are just as happy about your teammates' success as you are about your personal success. Just as Jesus relied on His disciples, we need our teammates and coaches to pursue goals successfully. Goals are never achieved alone; working together in unity ensures we stay on mission. Proverbs 27:17 reminds us that "as iron sharpens iron, so one man sharpens another." Strengthen one another with your words, actions, and attitude, knowing that when we work as one, we reflect the love of Christ and accomplish more than we ever could on our own.

On your team, I encourage you to begin to consistently hold "Put ups" or "Shout outs"—this is where teammates acknowledge other teammates with their effort and attitude at practice or in the game.

When I was coaching, I would have our team gather in a group after most practices and games and do what Frosty Westering called "attaways." An "attaway" would go something like this: "I want to give an attaway to Scotty Kessler for his never-giving-up attitude today. He started out walking a few guys and could have given up, but he hung in there and fought through and gave us three strong innings.

"Attaway, Kess!"

Notice how I didn't just give a "physical" acknowledgment but also a mental one, as Kess dug in deep and competed when things weren't going well. It is key to teach the mental and spiritual part of "attaways" and not just highlight who "performed well in the physical realm." It is okay to acknowledge physical contributions in a game or contest. However, make sure that isn't the only thing ever recognized. Our teams have created a great culture in these sessions after practice and games.

As you approach a game, match, or competition of any kind, realize that you will be displaying the Kingdom of God with the FOOT Principle. Be strategic about who fits into each of those categories. Who are the Forgotten, Opponents, Officials, and Teammates/Coaches?"

When we commit to blessing others, we embody the FOOT Principle: Bless your Forgotten, Officials, Opponents, and Teammates. This approach is how you create a team culture rooted in Christ's love, reflecting His heart for others in everything we do. A program that advances God's Kingdom starts with a foundation of blessing—seeing and serving those often overlooked, respecting officials, loving opponents, and building each other up as teammates and leaders.

This culture doesn't just create better athletes; it shapes disciples who carry God's light far beyond the field. By embracing the FOOT Principle, your team becomes a powerful example of God's love in action, making a lasting impact for His Kingdom.

Extending the FOOT Principle

This isn't only a field deal. This is a lifestyle. Hopefully, it becomes part of who you are. And who you are as a servant leader doesn't stop when you leave the team environment. It goes into Friday night, into the cafeteria, into when you're with your family at Thanksgiving. It's part of your DNA.

These principles are meant to be practiced as a lifestyle. They are God-honoring. They are God-glorifying. Even for individuals who don't care about God, they're people-enhancing; they're people-loving. They're not directed toward productivity; they are directed toward people. When you emphasize productivity, people get squashed. When you emphasize people, they become productive—not just on the field, but in all of life.

Discussion Questions

1. How can a team or coach create and sustain a culture of blessing in the competitive environment, particularly when facing tough competition or adversity?
2. What are some practical ways to "bless the forgotten" within a sports community (e.g., those not in the spotlight, such as bench players, officials, or staff), and how can this impact team dynamics and spiritual growth?

3. How does the concept of blessing opponents challenge the traditional mindset of rivalry and competition? What role does humility play in this shift?
4. In what ways can blessing officials during a game foster respect, discipline, and integrity in the competitive environment, and why is this crucial for reflecting Christ's character in sports?

CHAPTER 7

POUND THE ROCK: PRAYER AND THE PHILOSOPHY

*"Our praying needs to be pressed and pursued with
an energy that never tires, a persistency which will
not be denied, and a courage that never fails."*
E.M. Bounds

Next, we're going to take what might look like an alternative road and address prayer over the next two chapters—intentional, strategic prayer as it relates to this philosophy. There's a good reason for this. I haven't always felt this way; it hardly even used to cross my mind. Now, though, seeing more clearly, I believe there is a necessity to be intentional and strategic in prayer if we want this coaching philosophy to have the maximum impact the Lord would intend.

The Scriptures say, in 1 John 5, that if you pray according to His will, He hears you, and if you know that He hears you, you know you have received the request made of Him (1 John 5: 14–15, my paraphrase). That's a pretty bold promise! The caveat would be: what is His will?

We know that it's His will that all people be saved. It says He wants *all* to be saved and come to the knowledge of the truth (1 Timothy

2:3–6). It's His will that they be sanctified, be washed in the blood, and be cleansed by the Word of God for the forgiveness of their sin. It's His will that people be Spirit-filled, that we be submissive to God and to authority figures as appropriate. It's sometimes His will that we suffer; we learn obedience by suffering—even Jesus did (Hebrews 5:8). In fact, James 1:2 says we should count it all joy when we encounter suffering of many kinds.

We know that To-By-For is His will, so we can pray aggressively that we would play and coach and spectate according TO His Word, BY His power, and FOR His glory. He's going to answer those requests because that's His will!

What Happens When We Pray

What that looks like, how that plays out is at some level, is mysterious, like Hebrews 11. The men and women depicted in that passage, sometimes called the "Hall of Fame" chapter, they all were considered faithful and honored. Some were considered heroes and others were unknown, tortured, and killed. All were faithful.

Their outcomes were completely different. According to the world standards, some guys lost, and some guys won. However, God came in with a different way to think about it: they *all* won. They all won big, bigger than can even be communicated. What does this have to do with sport? It comes back to: we know that when we pray, according to God's will, He hears us and when we know that He hears us, we know that we have received the request made to Him. His will is that this biblical philosophy would prosper; we believe that sincerely because the root system is the Word of God, and the Spirit of God, and the target is His glory.

This means we can pray aggressively—not in terms of the scoreboard, but that the outcomes would be for His glory, His way, His will. Prayer is the piece that, when connected with the Word of God, produces this power and result. People coming to faith and growing in the faith. People becoming disciples of Jesus, who then make disciples, within the context of sport.

Now, the devil is looking to steal, kill, and destroy; Jesus has come to bring abundant life (John 10:10). We, as humans, and the visible world, are playing out this invisible battle that has visible impact and eternal ramifications. Prayer is one of our divinely powerful weapons in this battle! Though we are flawed humans, who once were lost but now are found, whose identity used to be as sinners and now is as saints, we are sons and daughters of God. This is all part and parcel of the philosophy: our identity in Christ.

The bottom line is this. This philosophy of competing biblically goes against every aspect of my natural inclination and my flesh. I want to win. I want to be in charge. I want to be glorified. Now, I might have some slightly more noble aspirations than that, but as the Bible reminds us, our flesh is desperately wicked (Jeremiah 17:9, KJV). All have sinned and fall short of the glory of God (Romans 3:23), and the wages of sin is death (Romans 6:23). But if we confess Jesus is Lord and believe in our heart God raised Him from the dead, we can be saved (Romans 10:9). This is the gospel message. "This is the will of God: for all men to be saved and to come to a knowledge of the truth" (1 Timothy 2:4).

Battling the Flesh

There is resistance in our old inclination, where we want to win; we have to put that to death. We're battling our own flesh. Even if we believe this philosophy, every day, still, when we're competing, coaching, or watching sports, we have to battle our desire for our will instead of His will. We have to aggressively, with our mouth, confess the truth over and over. "We want Your will, Your way, Your power, Your goals, Your desires, Your glory, Your glory, Your glory, God! Not our will, but Yours be done!" This is the fabric of the *Competing Biblically* philosophy. It doesn't work without this.

We are attempting to run head-on into the world, against the world's ways—and, frankly, some of the Christian world's thinking about sport. There is tremendous resistance. My own story in Chapter 1 is great testimony to how the battle of our own flesh is put on display.

If you want to see the power of God, you yourself will need to be a vehicle of intercession, standing between God and man, standing between light and darkness. There are two kingdoms, the kingdom of light and the kingdom of darkness. Sport is a battleground that, as much as anything, plagues our flesh. There is success and failure, humiliation and worship of man. There are all kinds of things on the table in the sport context. Whether you're four years old or 60, there are trophies and awards. Athletes are elevated and celebrated. They are focusing on outcomes that have to do with the exaltation of man, which has to do with pride and ego, which play on our flesh.

But if we belong to Jesus, the Spirit of God and the Word of God are weapons that are not of this world (see 2 Corinthians 10:3–5). They destroy strongholds of selfishness, ego, pride, and rebellion. The stronghold has to be attacked by weapons that are not of this world. Prayer and the Word of God are the lighter fluid and dynamite, which bring the power of God, and the Word of God, and the glory of God, into the sports setting.

This is not just a spiritual conversation; it's actually very practical. My contention is, if you want to see the supernatural power that is possible within this philosophy manifested in the transformation of lives for eternity—for evangelism, discipleship, deeper and deeper commitment for anybody, individually—the only way this can happen is through prayer and the Word of God. I would argue that not only is this philosophy impossible without the Spirit of God, but you're also not even going to scratch the surface unless intercessory prayer—unless quantity with quality—is part of the fabric of your athletic community.

That's my conviction: that prayer is at the beginning and end of the process—every game, every player, every interaction immersed in biblical prayer, prayer with the Word of God, praying the Scriptures. That the fruit of the Spirit—love, joy, peace, patience, kindness, goodness, faithfulness, gentleness, and self-control—would be manifested. That prayer would not be just part of the process but driving the process. It is the critical mass that brings about the explosion. How do you know it's critical mass? When it explodes!

If you want to see impact, and you have not made a costly investment into intercessory prayer for God to change you and change the participants and observers and the fabric of society as an interactive sport, you may see good things, you may see great things, but you won't see the impact that the Spirit of God desires. The root system is driven by the Spirit of God and the Word of God. Unless you are committed to intercessory prayer, you may see progress, you may see good things. But, if you want the supernatural, if you want generational, transformational impact, if you want a legacy that touches the world, not just your little team; if you want results that accomplish the will of God for the world, and reaching the world for the gospel, then you'd better have tapped into the power of prayer.

Why don't people do this? Why won't people consider offering more than just a casual rote prayer, if that? I call that kind of prayer a "butter knife." A butter knife is a knife, right? But a scalpel has a whole different level of impact. A butter knife can help butter bread. A scalpel is used for surgery. A scalpel can save lives. A scalpel can transform lives. Both are knives, but they're two entirely different things. Unless you know and understand intercessory prayer, like a scalpel with an intentional, strategic plan of implementation, you're going to have butter-knife impact. A butter knife is nice, but there's more out there. The possibilities are bigger and wider and deeper and higher. This philosophy is that. The key that unlocks that is biblical prayer—prayer with the Word of God.

The same reasons people don't use the *Competing Biblically* philosophy are the same reasons people don't tap into the power source of prayer. Why don't people tap into this power? Here are some of the reasons:

1. *Ignorance.* They've never heard it articulated. This is a critical component.
2. *Unbelief.* They've never seen it done and are skeptical that it works. They don't think they have to pray that way.
3. *Fear of man.* People fear what other people will think if they commit to that kind of intercession for God to grab hold of players, coaches, cities, and countries.
4. *Time cost.* There's no substitute for the time of intercession it requires to produce a man or woman of God who will walk with God for a lifetime, finish strong, reproduce, and multiply. Those kinds of people are rare. They are as rare as the prayer it takes to produce those kinds of transformational outcomes and individuals—vertically with God and horizontally with their fellow humans.

A few years ago, I established a prayer guide to walk us through some of the points of the *Competing Biblically* philosophy. At one point, we were talking about the philosophy for 45 minutes and praying for 15 minutes. I had the thought to flip the switch on that approach and talk the philosophy for 15 minutes and pray the philosophy for 45 minutes. Priorities! For me, personally, the Lord began to develop the philosophy within my heart.

This was our practice. There is no magic formula within the prayer. We simply pray the Scripture listed and pray that we would fulfill the attributes of the *Competing Biblically* approach. We pray the Scripture out loud and believe Jesus to help us walk in the power of His Word.

A Tale of Two Victories

I want to tell you two different stories passed down to me through Scotty Kessler that illustrate the fruit we see coming out of the culture of competing biblically or, as Frosty Westering would say, "More Than Winning." If you are familiar with Frosty and the remarkable comebacks and turns of events in any given game his PLU Lutes played in, you will not be shocked to hear about this one. However, this is the most incredible tale I have heard from that storied program.

During a season when Kess was an assistant coach under Frosty, a game was played on a beautiful Pacific Northwest Saturday afternoon in 1995 that saw Pacific Lutheran University go up against the talented Willamette University in the end-of-year conference championship game. Willamette controlled the game for almost four quarters, much to the chagrin of PLU fans. However, with the never-say-die Lutes and Frosty on the PLU sideline, the Lutes, as usual, felt like they had a chance.

As the clock dwindled down to just under four minutes, the PLU boys found themselves down 35 to 15 with the ball on their own 20-yard line and no time-outs. The game looked like it would end as an apparent blowout game. On first down from their own 20-yard line, with 3:58 left on the clock, a trick play turned into an 80-yard score that quickly closed the gap to 35–22. There was a turnover by Willamette, another PLU touchdown, an onside kick recovered, and then finally a 60-yard Lute touchdown drive that ended with a catch and fumble in the endzone to tie the game as time ran out. The PAT would be the clinching point to send Frosty and the Lutes to the next round in the playoffs. PLU missed the PAT to keep the game at 35–35 (there were no overtime rules back then).

The Lutes, down 35 to 15 with under four minutes, no time-outs, and the ball on their own 20, somehow scored 20 unanswered points and the game ended in a tie. That result made PLU higher ranked than Willamette and they made it into the playoffs the following week—amazing and miraculous, to say the least! Frosty and the Lutes pulled off the impossible again!

Leading up to that game, Kess had felt led to do a complete fast from all food for 10 days, and sensed the Lord say to him that there would be a powerful move of God within the game. Now, we are not saying that fasting and prayer made the miraculous result occur. We are not preaching a prosperity gospel of "if you do this, then good things will happen." We know that persecution and heartache can come after fasting and praying, just as much as victories. However, Kess felt led to quiet his heart and spirit and seek God during the two weeks preceding that game. Kess obeyed what he felt like was a leading from the Lord to fast and pray for a move of God during the game, regardless of what "victory" might entail. He simply sensed that there would be some kind of holy outcome within the context of the game. In this case, there happened to be a victory on the scoreboard. The greater victory was that God manifested a supernatural and miraculous experience.

As they left the field that day, Willamette was stunned, the crowd was stunned, and at some level, PLU was stunned! There was a "What just happened?" atmosphere that comes when something miraculous happens before your eyes. However, the head coach of all head coaches wasn't stunned. After all, the same God was the One who set the stage for the greatest miracle of all time with His own Son's resurrection! This game had a resurrection feel to it. Once again, the Lutes showed that competing as more than champions was who they were and not what they did.

The next tale of "victory" came while Coach Kessler was at Greenville College, and it had a decidedly different outcome. Kess had a sense that God was asking him to do something different leading up to the game with their upcoming opponent, Wheaton College of Illinois. However, on this occasion he was the head coach of the team rather than one of the assistants.

He wanted to do a prayer walk from the cafeteria to the field before the pre-game warm up. He asked the players who wanted to participate to join him.

Kess had been recently inspired while reading the biblical account of the army of Israel going into war, singing and worshipping God (2 Chronicles 20). Although it may have seemed silly to some, he told the team he wanted to sing worship songs while walking to the field as part of the prayer walk. He let them know that if they did not want to participate, to walk at the end of the line and be respectful.

The team bought in with Coach Kess. They did the prayer walk from the cafeteria to the field, which was about a quarter of a mile. However, the team did not stop singing worship songs once they got to the field. They took their concert into the locker room, where they continued singing. Kess went to the field to walk and pray pre-game as the team was dressing and singing. He became emotional on the field as he listened to his team worship the King of Kings in the pre-game locker room.

The Greenville team would be going up against a very good and ranked Wheaton team. It was truly a David-versus-Goliath scenario. On the first drive, Wheaton fumbled, and Greenville recovered and scored quickly. Fresh off their singing and worship, Greenville was up 7 to 0. Could this be another miraculous outcome from the Lord? Well, yes and no.

Wheaton went on to score the next 60 points and won 60 to 7 that Saturday afternoon. However, a miracle did occur, despite the numbers on the scoreboard. The Greenville team was united all afternoon. They fought hard and performed chants of encouragement from the sidelines throughout the game. Some of the players continued to sing worship songs during the game on the sideline. They were a true team. Every time Wheaton scored, which was often, they did not show discouragement or letdown. They hustled after every play. They showed true grit and determination playing to the whistle.

Now, here is where victory lies. Kess believed once again that he would see a great victory and a great move of God that day. The victory did in fact occur. The chain gang on the sideline that day (the chain gang is usually on the visitors' sideline, and they were in this game as well), and wanted to talk to Coach Kess after the game. They were older guys and had been doing the chain gang for the Wheaton College games for many years. They told Kess that they had never witnessed a sideline or visiting team like Greenville in all their years. They were astounded at the grit, the never-say-die mentality in the midst of getting blown out, the way players encouraged one another, blessed each other with cheers, chants, and even singing. The chain gang was blessed as Greenville fulfilled the call to be a blessing during all situations, even losses.

The reason why the display of courage stood out to the chain gang is because 99 percent of the time, when a team is losing that badly, they do not display that type of behavior. A miracle happened that day! A victory did happen that day! The Kingdom of God was displayed, and love of teammates and courage were displayed despite being outmatched physically by a superior opponent.

Some people think you have to win a game to have a testimony. While there may be truth to that at some degree, it wasn't the case that Saturday afternoon. The fans saw the Kingdom, the chain gang saw the Kingdom, and most importantly, we believe the King watched His Kingdom displayed in triumph.

Coach Kess considered that game a pivotal moment for the program. He believed an internal change occurred, transforming the team's identity from that point throughout the rest of the season. Competing biblically became their essence, not just their actions, confirming the principle that internal changes precede external displays.

So, in the "Tale of Two Victories," one is on the scoreboard for the world to see, and one is in the heart for the world to see. In both cases, victory belongs to the Lord!

Discussion Questions

1. *Intentional Prayer and Philosophy:* How does intentional, strategic prayer align with the *Competing Biblically* philosophy? In what ways can prayer enhance the impact of a sports team's spiritual growth and unity?

2. *Battle of the Flesh:* In this chapter, we talked about the internal battle between our flesh and the desire to honor God's will. How do we recognize and address our own fleshly desires in the context of competition, coaching, or spectating?

3. *Power of Prayer in Sports:* We talked about the significance of intercessory prayer for transformative results in sports. How can a coach or athlete practically implement more intentional prayer into their training, games, or team environment?

4. *Victory beyond the Scoreboard:* The stories of the PLU and Greenville College teams highlight the concept of "victory" beyond winning on the scoreboard. How can we redefine success in sports to include spiritual growth, teamwork, and glorifying God, even in the face of defeat?

CHAPTER 8

"Q OVER Q"
THE QUANTITY OF FORCE OVER
THE QUANTITY OF TIME

"Spiritual work is taxing work, and men are loath to do it. Praying, true praying, costs an outlay of serious attention and of time, which flesh and blood do not relish."
E.M. Bounds, *Power through Prayer*

I want to continue to talk about prayer, because I believe it is, to borrow a phrase from Reggie Jackson, "the straw that stirs the drink" of the well that never runs dry. There are numerous major points we hope you will consider as a coach of any age group, team, or program. The chief among them is to pray together as a coaching staff. One man puts to fight one thousand; two men put to fight ten thousand. Where one person prays, we know God is there. When people pray together, things change. Laying hands on others, anointing with oil, or fasting combined with prayer, creates unique and powerful effects.

I cannot overemphasize my encouragement for you to radically commit yourself to prayer, to tithe your time. Regardless of how many hours you work each day, there will always be enough time remaining to give some to the Lord. This is about the heart of the issue. Working harder or working longer is not going to help you turn the corner when it comes to God. You are better off working less and praying more. Ask any believer and they would agree, at least philosophically, but there is a gigantic gap in the practical expression of that ideal. The more you read and study biblical examples of prayer, the clearer that truth becomes.

God Moves through Prayer

There is a correlation between intentional, committed prayer, and moving long term with God. Evangelism doesn't end when people raise their hands for the first time on Sunday. To move with God long term is to be saved, be filled with the Spirit, multiply, and then finish strong. These are conversions that are trackable over decades.

C.T. Studd, a missionary to China, India, and Congo, did not even count conversions unless the converts were walking with God with fruit ten years later. We take the measurable numbers after one rally, even though the parable of the seed says there will be seeds snatched by birds, choked by weeds, and roots that will not take hold.

When groups of people find the Lord, there are always some who remain lost. They may have raised their hand, but they are lost. Only the fourth seed is the one that bears fruit and multiplies. This is the long-term fruit with long-term impact and long-term sustainability; we produce born-again people. Those don't happen automatically, just as the parable of the seed shows.

You can pray by yourself. But praying with others has something more and different. Do you? On a regular basis? We call that "long praying"—praying for an hour or more at a time in a somewhat regular pattern. When Jesus was talking to the disciples at Gethsemane, and they fell asleep, He asked them, "Could you not pray for an hour?" (Mark 14:32-42, NIV) We are not trying to draw some doctrine about how an hour of prayer is better than 45 minutes. We are just saying to long pray, just as Jesus did in Mark 1:35, where He went off early in the morning, and prayed.

After the crucifixion, the disciples gathered, waited, and prayed for 10 days. Elijah was like us; the Apostle James reminds us in James 5:17 that he prayed to stop and start the rain. We have the ability to change the weather through prayer! Do you believe that? If we don't, we won't pray that way.

I know programs where coaches pray regularly together. I had a chance to visit Arizona Christian University, where a sports missionary, Randy Chambers, is doing an amazing job in impacting the athletic department and campus in evangelism, discipleship, and prayer. I was able to visit him and join him with a group of football coaches in a prayer meeting.

I witnessed football coaches laying prostrate on the ground with their face on the floor, crying out to God for the members and staff of their football program. It was an awesome sight to behold. It is not coincidence that hundreds of athletes have been baptized and given their lives to Jesus over the last decade on the Arizona Christian Campus. These people on the campus have been standing in the gap and interceding for every athlete that steps into the gym, fields, pool, and court. The incredible thing about their intercession is that it will continue on as arrows into eternity. There will be fruit for decades that come from those times laying prostrate on the ground and crying out to God.

We have seen programs where the coaches offer it up to players to participate in prayer. In 2002, a player by the name of Cole Espencheid was playing for Coach Kess at Greenville College. Kess invited the football team to join him in prayer after practice. Prior to this, Kess and a few other leaders on campus had decided to pray five days a week for an hour. They wanted to see a move of God occur on the campus. Cole started going to some of the prayer meetings and engaging in long praying. The impact on Cole's life in those prayer meetings would be transformational as he developed a heart for God and began to develop a taste of God's heart for his team, campus, country, and world. After his playing days in college, Cole was so impacted by his time of soaking in the Word of God and prayer that he went into full-time sports ministry. He is a prime example of the 20-year impact, as it has been just over 20 years since his introduction to the philosophy of living a To-By-For lifestyle.

Cole has impacted hundreds working with the Fellowship of Christian Athletes and Kingdom Sports Ministry. He has traveled across the United States putting on clinics, "Doing Sports God's Way," as well as spending time ministering internationally. We would contend that Cole's maturation and heart to see others discipled and follow Jesus was first born in the prayer room. We have also seen players who start their own prayer groups—more rare, but it's out there.

Reproduce and multiply intercessors the same way you make disciples. Intercession is not a spiritual gift. It's a commandment to pray. Jesus did it and the disciples asked to watch Him. They prayed and He watched them pray. Then He sent them out to reproduce what they had done, and the intercessors multiplied. This is the method we still follow to this day.

The idea of an individual making a difference is powerful. One person can inspire and lead a movement, but it takes many people to sustain it. An individual who encourages others to take action and follow their example can create a ripple effect that reaches far and wide.

Do you have a vision for making an impact, or do you prefer to focus on personal enjoyment? God's heart is for the world, and He wants to use us to reach the world. Evangelizing and discipling through sport is one of those opportunities.

Leaders Need Covering

Prayers for protection are so crucial. Everyone needs covering. Everyone needs prayer protection. For one, we know those who are leaders spiritually need covering because they are judged more harshly (James 3:1). Whether someone is the head coach, the head of a family, or the head of a country, by stepping out, they are inviting the powers of darkness to disable them. If you can get the leader, you get everything. Even in the natural world we can see that. If you can go after a private or go after a general, whom are you going to go after?

Here's the bottom line: if someone is a head coach, they are responsible for protecting their athletes, their flock, their team, their family. As they protect and cover their players, they are susceptible to the flaming powers of the evil one. The way it works, when it works right, is that the flock is praying for their leader, as the leader is covering them. They pray for their leader, so that the flaming arrows of the evil one will not penetrate their leader's armor. This is the culture we are trying to create. The head coaches pray for assistants. Assistant Coaches are praying for the head coach and one another. The Coaching Staff will pray for the team. It is powerful when members of the team gather and pray for the coaches. This is the culture of prayer.

We have to fight with the Word of God and prayer to bind and disable the darkness, because the little-g-god of this age has blinded the mind of the unbelievers—they can't see (2 Corinthians 4:4). Through prayer, we help restore sight to those who cannot longer see, as authorized by the Word of God and prayer. Our "weapons" are not of this world (2 Corinthians 10:4)!

Taking Ground for the Kingdom through Prayer

Prayer is not just our provision and protection. It's also meant to take ground in the name of the Lord. In the Old Testament, when the people of Israel came into Canaan, God said, "Take the land; I have given you the victory. You are my ambassadors. You are my representatives. Take the land! Sure, there are giants there. But I am with you!"

In our day, there's culture, there's peer pressure, there is the world—saying you must do it one way or you're a fool, and if all that is not enough, there's Satanic assault. And yet still God says, "Take the land!"

We are going to live eternally somewhere. Take ground! Take the land! You have everything you need. You have the Word of God. You have prayer. The God of the universe is inside your body. Out of your mouth, take the land. Testify, speak, bless, present the gospel! Lead people into relationships. All these things are part of the sport context.

The devil is trying to use sports to edify people and glorify their own names. We are playing sport to edify God and glorify His Name. Jesus died so that we can be reconciled to God and redeem what has been stolen. This is how we think about it, even for youth sports.

Those children and teens out on the field are going to either live forever in Heaven or hell. Whether our kids are on the team, or we know somebody on the team, they are a part of our community. Sport is what brings us together.

This is a titanic, invisible war. The Church can partner with sport to reach its city, its country, its world. It is a fight against darkness. You are not going to disable darkness when you just want to play by your own power, for your own glory. Impossible! You have to have the principle of perseverance.

Just take a look at a Bible concordance and see how many times the Scripture says, ". . . if you continue," or, ". . . if you endure," or, ". . . if you persevere." Matthew 7:7 says to ask and keep on asking. Seek and keep on seeking. Knock and keep on knocking.

How about the parable of the persistent widow? (Luke 18:1–8) She kept crying out for justice, despite her pleas seemingly falling on deaf ears. Yet she never gave up, and she was heard. The unjust judge said, "I am going to give her what she wants because she's bothering me." Wouldn't God who is good and who is for you be so much better than the unjust judge, who is changed by the woman who cried out continuously?

Pray and Keep Praying

This is what we mean when we talk about "pounding the rock," the title of the previous chapter. You pound a rock with a sledgehammer until you break it. I will tell you what the rock is, in this case: the philosophy of sport in the world. You will have to pound it with the Word of God and prayer, by how you play, how you coach, and how you watch sports.

You hit a rock a hundred times, and it breaks on the hundredth blow. Which blow is the most critical? The answer is all of them. Each and every hit was critical to allow for the breaking of that rock. Jeremiah 23:29 says, "Is not my word like fire, and like a hammer that breaks a rock to pieces." Keep pounding the rock!

If you want to break the rocks of selfishness, pride, ego, idolatry, if you want to break those rocks that are embedded in your family, team, or philosophy, you'll need to apply great force over a long time. We call that "Q over Q": the quantity of force over a quantity of time creates impact.

Quantity of force. Forceful praying. "The Kingdom of God is forcefully advancing, and forceful men and women take hold of it," Jesus said (Matthew 11:12). We might say they use scalpels and not butter knives! Stay at it. Do the right thing the right way and stay at it. Don't be discouraged if nothing changes. Don't be discouraged if nothing seems to have an impact. Don't be discouraged because we know what the Scriptures declare. Pray according to His will and He hears you (1 John 5:14–15). If you know He hears you and it's His will, you know you'll receive. From the moment you begin to pray, according to God's will, He hears you. The answer is on the way.

Sometimes something gets in the way; sometimes it's an invisible being, such as in Daniel 10. Sometimes it is a contest in the heavenlies, like Job experienced, a contest between Satan and God over Job and his family line. There is more going on there than you think. And until we commit to the Word of God and prayer, as a force of God, a weapon that is not of this world, we will not see transformational impact in sport or through sport.

This philosophy does not work by accident. It works on purpose, when people pray and act.

Prayer as a Part of Discipleship

Below is a part of our Discipleship Program we call the "Big 10." This part of the Big 10 Discipleship program emphasizes prayer. It provides instructions and advice on various forms and ideas of praying.

Why do we pray?

- For power: prayer is like oil to an engine
- To express a desire for a relationship with God
- For communication: like picking up a phone to talk to our Father
- To sow into what He wants to do with us
- To elicit a divine-human cooperative

We use the acronym TACOS. This is not meant to be a robotic way of praying but is a blueprint on how to get started. Remember, this is foundational for all:

T—Thanksgiving—thanking God for what He has done

A—Adoration—praising God for who He is

C—Confession—praying to God and acknowledging our sin

O—Others—praying to God for others

S—Self—praying to God for ourselves

Why TACOS? It helps us live out Psalms 100:4, "Enter his gates with thanksgiving and his courts with praise; give thanks to him and praise his name."

It is not necessary to pray TACOS in the same prayer progression. The person praying can choose to pray in order or outside of the acronym. The end goal with this prayer type specifically is a balanced prayer life.

If we are only praying thanksgiving, adoration, praise, and confession, we may forget that we are supposed to make requests of God (that He wants to meet our needs and the needs of others).

If we are never praying confession, we may forget that there is to be humility in prayer and we must have a clean heart to be "heard" by

God. If we are only praying intercession (prayers for others), we may forget that God asks us to ask things for ourselves. If only supplication, the danger is that our prayer life may be selfish. If praying only intercession and supplication, we may forget that prayer is not only "asking stuff" of God (as if His whole job is to "do things" for us), but that our prayer life is primarily to be in relationship with Him in reverence and humility . . . God speaking with us, and us speaking with Him.

The bottom line is that, in any prayer time, we might emphasize one kind of prayer over another due to a particular need or "season" in life. When praying, there should be a "heart connection," and we should enter into the presence of God. Additionally, we are encouraged to pray with a whole heart, a clear mind, a strong will, and great passion.

Developing an Individual Prayer Plan

1. When do you pray?
   - Morning/day/night (all of these are options, or one could be an option)
   - At a special time during the day
   - At selected times throughout the day
   - At regular intervals throughout the day
2. How do you pray?
   - Alone or with others
   - Journaling
   - Use the Bible as a "prayer manual"
   - Prayer walk (walk and pray)
   - Intercessory prayer
   - Listening prayer
3. What is your posture in prayer?
   - Standing, sitting, kneeling, or lying down
   - Raising your hands
   - Eyes open
   - Eyes closed

Discussion/Prayer Activity: Popcorn TACOS

This activity can be used with all ages and is designed to teach people how to pray. There will be processing questions near the end that should be used to reinforce the material. We call it "Popcorn Tacos."

Someone is designated to be the prayer leader. They will shift the group to the next letter in the TACOS acronym (when more than two are praying, each person will pray for the last however the Spirit moves them, or by using the TACOS model).

Popcorn Prayer Rules:

- Prayers are brief, one to three lines max (so no one dominates)
- No one prays consecutively (exception after gap of silence)
- Prayer "popcorns" around in the group until the leader closes

Discussion Questions

1. How does the concept of "Q over Q" (Quantity of Force over Quantity of Time) apply to your personal prayer life and the impact it has on long-term spiritual growth, both as a coach and as a believer?

2. What do you think is the significance of praying together as a coaching staff or team? How can this collective prayer shape the culture and impact of a team or program?

3. C.T. Studd emphasized long-term fruit from conversions. How can we, as coaches or leaders, ensure that the spiritual lives of our athletes and teams are sustained and not just momentary? What steps can we take to help others grow in their faith over time?

4. From the section about "Taking Ground for the Kingdom through Prayer," what are some specific ways you could use prayer to take ground within your team or sports community? How does this align with the mission of using sports for the glory of God?

SECTION 4

The Fruit of the Philosophy

CHAPTER 9

THEY COME TO BEAT US; WE COME TO BE US

"They come to beat us; we come to be us."
—Frosty Westering

"I am the vine; you are the branches. If a man remains in me and I in him, he will bear much fruit; apart from me you can do nothing."
—John 15:5

This quote by Frosty Westering is one of my all-time favorites. To me, it beautifully captures the essence of what it means to compete biblically. That's why I place it in the category we call "The Fruit of the Philosophy."

The fruit is the evidence—what others see. But the fruit is only possible when the root system is healthy and grounded in fertile soil. That root system must be anchored in the trunk of the tree, which represents prayer. From the trunk, branches grow outward as a display of what we can do as believers in Jesus. These are what we call the *branches of blessing*:

- Blessing the Forgotten
- Blessing the Opponent
- Blessing the Officials
- Blessing Teammates and Coaches

The fruit growing from those branches is the outcome of a transformed heart—a heart aligned with Christ. This fruit is truly the Fruit of the Spirit, which Wes Neal once called "The Nine Attitudes of the Athlete." Within our philosophy, we emphasize specific fruits as especially vital in the world of sports:

- Love
- Humility
- Servant leadership
- Competing against your best self (identity)

When coaches and athletes are transformed by Christ, they begin to operate in these fruits. Imagine playing or coaching with a spirit of **love, joy, peace, patience, kindness, goodness, gentleness, faithfulness**, and **self-control** (see Galatians 5:22–23). Some might see these traits as signs of weakness or a "soft" mentality. But we believe the opposite is true.

When your spiritual eyes are opened—when you fully understand *who you are* and more importantly, *whose you are*—you'll experience a boldness and intensity unlike anything else. It becomes an all-out, never-quit mindset. This is not because of what you do, but because of *who you are*. This is the fruit of the philosophy, brought to life in action.

We now carry the nature of Christ—the same Christ who determined to go to Jerusalem and lay down His life for humanity. That's the ultimate act of love. The ultimate humility. Jesus left the throne of Heaven to become a servant and ransom for many. He modeled the perfect Servant Leader, the one who laid down His life first. And He knew His identity. He didn't compare Himself to others. He knew His mission and He knew the plan.

We pray that you come to know *who you are*: a blood-washed child of God, filled with the same Holy Spirit who raised Jesus from the grave. You carry His love, His humility, His servant leadership, and His identity.

This is *who we are*.

We must know this in our gut, in our spirit. We must keep pounding the gospel and the principles of *Competing Biblically* into our hearts so we can live out this truth. The expectation is not just that we bear fruit, but that we bear fruit that *lasts*.

Let's explore what each fruit means—and how it shapes us as athletes, coaches, and parents.

Fruit 1: Love

The fruit on a tree isn't for the tree itself or even its branches. Fruit is meant to be picked, eaten, and enjoyed by others. It's the outward display of the tree's health and life. In the same way, the fruit of the Competing Biblically philosophy is the visible evidence of the Kingdom of God in and through us. Psalm 34:8 invites us: "Taste and see that the Lord is good." That should be the experience of those who encounter us in coaching, playing, or spectating—there should be a sweet aroma and taste of God's goodness through our lives.

As coaches, athletes, and leaders, we are called to treat people with the fruit of the Spirit—love, joy, peace, patience, kindness, goodness, faithfulness, gentleness, and self-control. Even if people don't recognize the source, they'll recognize the fruit. I can love God, love people, and love the game—and compete with incredible passion and focus—because I've been given supernatural fuel that those without Christ don't have access to. When that love manifests, it brings blessing instead of destruction.

Sure, anger can be a motivator, but it's not sustainable. People get hurt along the way. Love, on the other hand, is stronger than hate. It conquers hate. The Holy Spirit fills us with supernatural love: love for people, love for the game, love to work out, love to prepare, love to bless others, love to play, love to practice. This is not natural—it's supernatural.

Even in the context of intense, physical sports, the fruit of the Spirit is still accessible. Competing biblically doesn't mean compromising physicality. Jesus-centered athletes can be both fierce and loving.

We see testimonies of God-driven, elite athletes who are both highly competent and deeply rooted in Christ.

At the heart of biblical coaching is love—love for God, love for others, and love for the game. As Mark 12:30–31 says: " 'Love the Lord your God with all your heart and with all your soul and with all your mind and with all your strength . . . Love your neighbor as yourself.' " Love is not merely a feeling—it's a guiding principle that shapes every decision a coach makes.

Jesus said in John 13:34–35: "A new command I give you: Love one another. As I have loved you, so you must love one another. By this everyone will know that you are my disciples if you love one another." In coaching, that love looks like investing in your athletes' lives, caring about their well-being, and encouraging their growth—not just as players, but as people.

And what does love look like from the players? It's how they treat each other, their coaches, the opposing team, officials, staff, and everyone else involved in the sport. First John 4:7–12 reminds us: "Dear friends, let us love one another, for love comes from God. Everyone who loves has been born of God and knows God . . . because God is love." Love is the foundation that every other branch of biblical coaching grows from.

Whether you're a coach, athlete, team, or organization—the world will know we belong to Christ by our love for one another.

Fruit 2: Humility

Humility is the second essential fruit in our tree analogy. Philippians 2:3–4 instructs us: "Do nothing out of selfish ambition or vain conceit. Rather, in humility value others above yourselves, not looking to your own interests but each of you to the interests of the others." Biblical humility means putting others—your athletes, your team—before yourself. It's not about personal glory, but about serving the greater good.

First Peter 5:5–6 also speaks to this: "Clothe yourselves with humility toward one another, because, 'God opposes the proud but shows favor to the humble.' . . . Humble yourselves, therefore, under God's mighty hand, that he may lift you up in due time." Peter may have had Jesus washing his own (Peter's) feet in mind when writing that. That act of servant-hearted humility is our example.

Humility isn't weakness—it's strength. It allows coaches to lead with integrity and to earn the trust of their athletes. It's essential for spiritual and relational growth. Humility keeps us teachable—both vertically (with God) and horizontally (with people). On the horizontal plane, we engage in evangelism (with non-believers) and discipleship (with believers). But both require humility.

Kess told me he remembers Dr. Coleman, author of *The Master Plan of Evangelism,* and his mentor in discipleship. would say, even in his late eighties, "Scotty, there's so much more to learn!" He wasn't just being polite—he meant it. The more he learned, the more he realized how much he didn't know. That's true humility. Men like Dr. Coleman and Billy Graham modeled that humility—and the impact of their lives continues around the world.

True humility must be paired with conviction. Our strength comes from the Lord. Our competence comes from Christ. Seeking wisdom and knowledge in order to serve well—that's the posture we need, whether we're on staff or laypeople. It's about servant leadership. Dying to self. Giving your life away—and realizing that in doing so, you actually receive more in return. Teachability matters.

We use the acronym **FATC** to describe the kind of people who are worth investing in—those who will multiply: *Faithful, Available, Teachable, Courageous.* As coaches, we know the difference between a teachable player and one who isn't. Pride creates a wall and resists the Spirit of God. Pride and rebellion go hand in hand. But humility opens the door to God's power. And here's the thing: people can smell pride. Even when we don't see it in ourselves, others often do. That disconnect hinders our relationships and our effectiveness. Pursuing humility is a willful act—we choose to humble ourselves before God, or He will do it for us. I'd much rather humble myself.

God is faithful to finish the work He's begun in us—and His desire is for us to walk in humility. Coaches want teachable players. Players want humble coaches. Parents want their kids to be humble. And kids are looking for parents who will say things like, "I was wrong. Please forgive me." That kind of humility is what makes everything work.

Think of it like a car engine. Gas (God's power and love) gets it moving, but without oil (humility and the Spirit's guidance), it breaks down. You need both. Being faithful, available, teachable, and courageous all contribute to being a valuable servant in the Kingdom.

"Humility is the mark of greatness." That means staying teachable, both vertically and horizontally. Galatians 6:3 warns us: "If anyone thinks they are something when they are not, they deceive themselves." A doctrinal study on humility would yield a wealth of Scripture—because it's essential to the life of faith.

Moses was known as a humble man—and he was called a friend of God. From the very beginning, humility has been part of God's call for His people. And it's something we must model and pass on.

Discipleship is a process:

- *I do it.*
- *I do it, you watch.*
- *You do it, I watch.*
- *You do it.*

That same process applies to humility:

- *I walk in humility.*
- *You watch me walk in humility.*
- *I watch you walk in humility.*
- *You walk in humility.*

Then you multiply it. Humility must be taught and modeled at every level.

Fruit 3: Servant Leadership

The world leads through **lordship**—top-down pressure and authority. But **servant leadership** is bottom-up. It isn't about controlling others but empowering them. It's not telling people what to do; it's inviting them to ask you questions about who you want to become. This is accountability rooted in humility, not dominance.

Instead of saying, "I'm going to hold you accountable to make sure you read or pray," ask, "How can I serve you? How are you doing in humility, in serving others, or in the fundamentals? How's your ministry? Where are you struggling?" This is the Spirit-led model Jesus gave us: *He came to serve, not to be served* (Mark 10:45). He laid down His life—and calls us to do likewise.

Frosty Westering coined the term "servant warriors." These weren't captains who controlled others—they led by serving. The world recognizes this as powerful. People want to follow a leader who puts their needs first. I remember a boss who cared more about my growth than I did. That motivated me to serve him. That's how it is with God: We are compelled by His love to live and die for the sake of others (2 Cor. 5:14–15).

Leaders go first and go farther. Like Medal of Honor soldiers who ran into fire knowing they'd likely die—they led by example. One man took a machine gun nest by sheer perseverance, inspiring his squad to follow. He could've stayed safe but chose to take more ground. That's a Kingdom principle: *God gives victory, but we must still fight.* God says, "I've given you the land—now go and take it." That means sacrifice. Some will live in caves; some will die. But each of us is called to obedience.

Like in John 21 when Peter asked about John's path, and Jesus said, "I'm talking to you," we must recognize that each has their price to pay. All of us are called to lead by serving—marked by humility.

Fruit 4: Competing Against Your Best Self—Knowing Your Identity

Galatians 6:4–5 says we should test our actions and take pride in personal growth, not comparing ourselves to others. Corinthians 10:12 specifically warns against measuring ourselves against others.

"They come to beat us, we come to be us." Frosty's phrase captures this principle. Others try to win; we try to close the gap between our **potential** and **performance**. This mindset keeps us in the zone. It's not about them—it's about becoming our best selves. We adjust to opponents but don't center on them. They are partners in competition, not enemies.

In this way, comparison kills growth. When I wanted to play, I hoped my teammate would fail so I could get more reps. That mindset creates division. You can't compete *against* your teammates for 355 days and expect *unity* on game day. Yet this is the norm in sports—offense vs. defense, starters versus backups. But when players slander or discourage one another, it destroys synergy

Synergy, on the other hand, is biblical—one puts 1,000 to flight, two put 10,000 (Deuteronomy 32:30). God multiplies what's surrendered. Five loaves of bread and two fish fed 20,000. The power of God elevates the ordinary when tied to obedience. The opponent is not our enemy—our real battle is the flesh.

This leads to personal responsibility. Satan can tempt us, but he doesn't make us sin—we choose. The old self is dead; we are born again. Competing biblically means dying to self, playing for God's glory, and closing the gap between who we are and who God's called us to be.

The comparison game leads to no wins. If I win only because my teammate fails, everyone loses. But when we serve one another, especially those who play less or are younger, we reflect Christ. You bless teammates pre- and post-practice. You reset your mindset like a thermostat—not reacting like a thermometer. That's having a clear mind, strong will, whole heart, and great passion.

When this mindset becomes culture, it flips the norm. Instead of competition creating division, it creates unity. We don't taunt, mock, or humiliate. Fear and hate can motivate, but not sustainably. That culture might produce short-term results—but not lasting joy, growth, or transferability off the field. It won't work in marriage or life. A person trained to dominate won't naturally switch to serve. You can't go from wanting to be #1 to becoming #9—the servant.

I've heard this called "the doctrine of depravity." Without Christ, we're self-absorbed. Sports magnify that, bringing out both the best and worst of us. But when surrendered to the Spirit, God redeems it. He brings order, power, and purpose.

Competing Biblically is about closing the gap between potential and performance—individually and corporately—by serving others and setting the thermostat. It's sustainable, reproducible, and multiplies. It blesses the team. It glorifies God. And it transforms lives.

Four Fruits Verse Bank

A Biblical Foundation for Christ-Centered Coaching

1. LOVE
The Call: Love God fully and love others deeply

Mark 12:30–31
"Love the Lord your God with all your heart and with all your soul and with all your mind and with all your strength . . . Love your neighbor as yourself."

John 13:34–35
"Love one another. As I have loved you, so you must love one another . . . By this everyone will know that you are my disciples."

1 John 4:7–12
"Dear friends, let us love one another, for love comes from God . . . God is love . . . Since God so loved us, we also ought to love one another."

1 John 4:18

"There is no fear in love. But perfect love drives out fear . . . The one who fears is not made perfect in love."

2. HUMILITY

The Call: think less of self and more of others

Philippians 2:3–4

"Do nothing out of selfish ambition . . . Rather, in humility value others above yourselves."

1 Peter 5:5–6

"Clothe yourselves with humility . . . God opposes the proud but shows favor to the humble."

3. SERVANT LEADERSHIP

The Call: lead by serving others with love

Mark 10:45

"The Son of Man did not come to be served, but to serve, and to give his life as a ransom."

Romans 12:10

"Be devoted to one another in love. Honor one another above yourselves."

Galatians 5:13

'Serve one another humbly in love."

4. COMPETE AGAINST YOUR BEST SELF

The Call: aim for excellence without comparison

Galatians 6:4–5

"Test your own actions . . . take pride in yourself alone . . . carry your own load."

2 Corinthians 10:12

"When they measure themselves by themselves and compare themselves with themselves, they are not wise."

Discussion Questions

1. *"They come to beat us; we come to be us."* What does this quote mean to you in the context of competition, and how does it shift your perspective on winning and identity?

2. *Love as visible fruit:* In what ways can love be shown during competition—toward teammates, opponents, officials, or even spectators? Share an example where you've seen or experienced this kind of love in action.

3. *The power of humility:* Why is humility so difficult in competitive environments? How can a coach or athlete cultivate humility without losing their edge?

4. *Rooted identity:* How does knowing your identity in Christ affect the way you approach competition, leadership, or adversity

CHAPTER 10

WINNING DEFINED

"Winning is the total release of all that you are toward becoming like Jesus Christ in each situation."
Wes Neal

"The peace of mind which is a direct result of self-satisfaction in knowing you did your best to become the best that you are capable of becoming."
John Wooden

We will now enter an area where there may be a little, possibly a lot, or total disagreement with our approach to winning and the scoreboard within the philosophy of *Competing Biblically*. We would only ask you to read through the philosophy and see where your heart may lead you. At first, I too was skeptical of his approach to winning and losing within the *Competing Biblically* philosophy.

However, over the years of hearing it from Scotty Kessler and seeing it in action with various programs, I have come to fully believe in this approach to winning. In fact, I would say that it was a key component of making me a better coach. I coached more freely, and I believe I closed the gaps in my coaching to bring me up to my full potential.

I am not perfect in the approach, but I am aiming for perfection in coaching freely.

I also want to add some context, with full humility and not proclaiming our accomplishments as players and coaches. Scotty Kessler is in five Halls of Fame as a player and a coach. He has won national championships as both a player and a coach. I am in two Halls of Fame as a player and in one Hall of Fame as a coach. I say that to make the point that you can have this philosophy of sport and still have "success." We have mentioned Frosty Westering many times throughout this book—he was also a proponent of this approach to winning. His record speaks for itself as the twelfth-winningest coach of all time in college football, with four national championships.

You don't necessarily have to agree with the philosophy, but you cannot say it doesn't work in terms of outcomes. We have coaches and athletes that would attest around the country that this approach to the scoreboard is effective—and brings glory to God.

Winning and the Scoreboard

This is the real flash point for this philosophy, and particularly how people treat referees and opponents. I want to make one mention as to why, for me, I talk about "developing" rather than "training" players, and why I say "impact" rather than "influence."

I used to say excellence is the goal. I changed that. Now I talk about perfection and aiming for perfection, and I want to explain why. It's not wrong or right; it's just my conviction. "Excellence" is just way too gray— too subjective. What's excellent to you and what's excellent to me may be two different things. You can believe something's excellent, and someone may think that's mediocre. In a sense, excellent has been so overused that it can be muddy and doesn't give a clear distinction anymore.

The word "perfection," on the other hand, has no gray in it. Perfection is perfection. It's 10/10. Frankly, in baseball, you're an excellent hitter if you hit 3/10. But perfection is 10/10. The Scriptures talk about perfection. God says, "Be perfect as I am perfect." (Matthew 5:48) We understand this has to do with heart and attitude and not behavior; we "aim for perfection." (2 Corinthians 13:11) So philosophically, in our coaching, we use the phrase "aim for perfection." Again, that's a high expectation; there is no higher expectation than perfection! But we have to hold that in tension with being under God's grace. When you marry high expectations with high grace, it's not problematic.

I want to have high expectations for myself as a husband, father, friend, worker, athlete, coach, and fan. I want to be held accountable to high expectations—in my walk with God and in my walk with people. At every level I want to be held accountable for it. I don't want people criticizing me or being dogmatic, but I want them to biblically hold me accountable, which is to build me up. I'm giving them the right to ask questions. I'm giving them the right to say, "You said this, or you did this, are you sure you want to, it seems to be inconsistent with your confession . . ."

I want to be held accountable to the Word of God, not to people's opinions about the Word of God or about life. I want to be held accountable to the Word of God by people who care deeply about me and want me to become the person who I want to become. This is the accountability we're trying to reproduce and multiply within the sports world, and also in the Christian world. In life in general, we should be looking for people to hold us accountable for what the Scriptures say! That's why our terminology is "aim for perfection."

The goal is to glorify God. Fundamentally, this is the target. We say To-By-For: according TO the Word of God, BY the power of God , FOR the glory of God. The glory of God is that we live for the praise of His glory. We live to lift His Name high, that God would draw all men to Himself. That's our target; sport is the vehicle. Winning is not our target, not outcomes. It's process versus results.

Winning Is Not the Primary Goal

Not only that, winning is not even a secondary goal. Glorifying God is the primary goal. It's the only goal. The byproduct of it is a lot of things.

Outcomes are a byproduct, or a result, of people who play competently at a high level, meshed with whatever their talent mix is, people who consistently close the gap between their potential and their performance. This is, to us, what winning is. Winning isn't the scoreboard. The prize isn't the trophy. The ultimate prize is being with Jesus forever in eternity. We're running a race in such a way as to win that prize.

Now, are we also attempting to succeed on the scoreboard and win games? Yes, of course, but not as a primary goal. Frosty never even talked about winning. He never said, even when his teams were in the playoffs, "We must win this game." He just said, "Let's play as long as we can." He found terminology that diffused the issue of winning and losing in the scoreboard because he knew that the outcome of that philosophy is that, at the end of the day, it demotivates. It demotivates you because, in some scenarios, it actually prevents you from closing that potential/performance gap; in fact, it actually increases the gap between your performance and potential, because certain goals inhibit performance.

Paradoxically, the best way to reach the target is not to run toward your dreams, but to set and strive for smaller, more manageable goals. Even if you don't care about Jesus or Heaven or ultimate rewards, you should note that even many sports psychologists would say that if you focus on the results rather than the process, you compromise the process, which then compromises the results.

Frosty would say, "Dreams are something you can see but you can't touch. Goals are something you can touch today." He talked about goal setting (which are things you can touch today), accomplishments that put you on track toward your dream, whatever it is. That's a helpful articulation of the difference between a dream and a goal.

An athlete can work with a whole heart, strong will, clear mind, and great passion every day and it still might not happen, because there may be a limit of talent and circumstances. A person can't control those but, for sure, if that player doesn't take care of business today in terms of developing his body, mind, soul, emotions, and spirit, then the chances decrease that he's going to reach that goal today, or that dream tomorrow. So, with making the shift from dreaming to goal setting, you're bringing people back to what they can do today.

Common terminology in coaching nowadays is "the next play." The next shot. We use that example in golf. What is the most important shot in a golf game? It's the next one. It's not the last one. It's the next one. If you don't take care of the next one, you decrease the chances it's going to go well in the end.

That's why this philosophy focuses more on every moment of every day and every play. You want to take care of the process. You need to get good at the fundamentals.

If I want to be a godly man, and if that's my dream, then I must have goals that are in line with that dream. That means I'd better read regularly; we say daily. I'd better have a prayer plan to pray different kinds of prayers, and to pray long and short. I'd better have a Bible memorization plan. I'd better have a gospel presentation plan, a gospel invitation plan, a testimony plan, and an accountability plan. I'd better have a plan to feed myself; we call that learning: how to use a study Bible, to study the Bible. If you don't have a plan to daily hit those goals, then the chance you hit the target decreases. It doesn't mean you won't hit it. It just increases or decreases your chances, based on what you do today.

If I keep waiting to change my habits and choices, I can have that plan for a thousand years; the chances are slim that it's going to happen. But what I do today feeds into tomorrow. And the fascinating thing is, I've got to do it every day. And if I don't do it every day, it slows down the process, because we can't skip steps. We don't become strong overnight.

There Is No Magic Pill

The bottom line is that there's no fast way to achieve greatness. There's no fast way to be super mature. It's a daily progression of steps or goals that you reach that put you on track for that end result.

Frosty used to say, "If you want a magic pill, here's magic: Make A Greater Individual Commitment" to what you want to be perfect at. There's no magic pill but there is MAGIC. And the magic isn't some external force. It's you internally making a decision to Make a Greater Individual Commitment—to Bible reading. To Bible memory. To Bible study. To gospel presentation. Being a spouse. Being a mother or father. Being a friend. Being a worker. If you want to aim for perfection or be great at anything, you have to make a greater individual commitment now, and then again and again. Repeat the process.

Once again, winning is not a goal at all. It's off the table. Rather, it's a result or byproduct of a whole bunch of other factors, some of which we control, some of which we don't. What we can do is with our attitude, our effort, our heart, our mind, our will, we can intentionally— that means on purpose, strategically, with a plan—glorify God. We do this by giving our whole heart, a strong will, a clear mind, and great passion to apply ourselves at any given moment to the process, whether it's internal or external. This is the what and the why.

The "how" is what it looks like in the heat of battle, or in preparation for the heat of battle, in sports. That's our off-the-field preparation. That's what happens in our mind, in our emotions, in our will, in our spirit as we get it ready. That's what happens when we go to the practice field, whether it's in season or out of season. Whether it's in a small group or individual time. Whether it's private or whether it's an official practice. Whether it's a big practice or a small practice. All of this is *worship*. All of this is acknowledgment of God, His Word, His power, His glory. This is our practical expression of the *Competing Biblically* philosophy: **our goal is to glorify God by aiming for perfection, not by winning.**

Winning Is Being Your Best Self

Aiming for perfection is being the best you can be. It's being your very best self. You're comparing yourself to yourself, not to others, to separate or outside entities. It's between you and God.

And then, it's between the team and God. This doesn't mean everyone on the team is following Jesus, maturely or at all. It just means whoever the leadership is, whether at a Christian school (or youth organization) or secular, all these principles apply. If you're in a secular setting, you may just have to be wise in your articulation of it.

Some aspects are arguably universal. The 10 Commandments talk about principles that civil societies around the world support, such as honoring authority figures and respecting other people's possessions. You don't have to call them the 10 Commandments and cite Bible verses—which in some situations you can't do. You can rephrase them in a different way, and everyone would say, *That's a good thing!*

When I teach these concepts on a team, I say things like, "Do you want to be on a team where you have to lock your locker because somebody's going to steal your stuff? Are you going to be on a team where other guys and gals try to take your girlfriend or boyfriend away? Are you going to be on a team where people are using foul language and speaking poorly of their parents and how much they hate them?"

Everybody who is sane, in my opinion, will say, "We don't want to be part of that. Well then, what you're saying is, you're adhering to what the Bible calls the 10 Commandments!

So, even this philosophy, for example, respecting the referees, even though it's a biblical philosophy, is a good thing—in my opinion, it is a good thing in any civil society. And I didn't throw in the corresponding Bible verse when I state that. Respecting the game is a good thing. Caring for other people's best interest is a good thing. Helping other people reach their goals is a good thing. Being considerate is a good thing. These principles are all based on Bible verses; we're just rephrasing them.

Even in a secular setting, I would contend, such as in professional football, where it's about winning first and last, I would say, "Gentlemen, if that is where you want to get as an outcome, this is the best way to get there." And I wouldn't have to use any Bible verses, per se (though at that point you could).

"Faith-Driven" Doesn't Mean Soft

There is a stereotype out there that, if you're a faith-driven coach or athlete, you're "soft." I think these kinds of stereotypes are insane. Unfortunately, though, if some athletes are immature in their walk, they might believe that about themselves—that they've lost their toughness, they've lost their passion. How does that happen? The God of the Universe is living inside your body and wants to play through you! You think there's more power there? Not to mention energy and focus and passion and love?

Love is stronger than hate. Hate is not sustainable, and love is. So, you have everything you need to be all that you can be in the sport context with more gas than you've got a chance to use. A nuclear bomb has power; God is the source of ALL power. It's between His little finger and His thumb. You think if you had nuclear energy in you, that you would play more aggressively? Well, you have Someone infinitely stronger than that inside of you. You are definitely not "soft."

Don't be deceived by the world's philosophy. Don't be foolish about where the power is to close that gap between your performance and potential because everybody, even the people of the world, are attempting to close the gap between their potential and their performance. If you have Jesus in and with you, you have the supernatural gas to do that. And you can glorify God in the process.

Winning as a By Product

Winning games is a byproduct of aiming for perfection. I'm not saying we don't care about the outcomes. I'm saying that, compared to glorifying God, the outcomes seem so distant a priority that they hardly seem to matter.

I spent a ton of time as a coach in preparation for outcomes, so the team would operate according to the right scheme and the right fundamentals and the right techniques. Although I'm a Jesus follower, I was always trying to maximize my toolbox, technically and structurally and attitudinally, in terms of the game. Don't think I didn't care about the outcomes just because they were not my target.

Competence and aiming for perfection are key in every way, in the professionalism of our craft. This is critical to our testimony and it honors God. The businessman is just as holy as the pastor. They simply have different roles, different relationships. Business can be worship as much as the work a pastor does. They're different roles with different responsibilities. But worship is foundational whether you're in full-time ministry or not.

We need to have high expectations with our craft. We need to have high expectations with our walk. And we must give high grace in both regards. Winning games is a byproduct of aiming for perfection; the outcomes are the result of a process. And that process is driven according TO the Word of God, BY the power of God, FOR the glory of God—"To-By-For." We care very much about it, and, at the same time, we don't care at all. In the same way that Jesus says we need to hate mother, father, sister, brother, children, etc., speaking hyperbolically of course, for the sake of Christ (Luke 14:26), we can apply this to sports. Do I hate winning? No, of course not. I'd much rather win than lose. But compared to His glory, I hate winning. Can you see that distinction? It's a supernatural distinction.

Run the Race to Win the Prize

We bring glory to God by running the race in such a way as to win the prize—running the race with a whole heart, clear mind, strong will, and great passion (1 Corinthians 9:24).

From the world's perspective, seeking God's glory or God's power or the Word of God is not on the table at all. If they're wise and human, they want to win. Yet, even within that framework, most generally understand the best way to get there is to focus on process, not results. That's a known philosophy within the competitive world. Now, I'm not saying everyone holds that position. They may say, "Process over results," but they really emphasize winning. That can be problematic for the process, though.

To invoke another Frosty-ism, "The goal is the road, not the end of the road." That was his way of saying process. He'd say to enjoy the trip. Don't get fixated on the destination. If you just want to get there, and you don't enjoy the trip, you waste a ton of time. In sport, the destination is the scoreboard. If you've spent hundreds of days each year aiming for the destination, and the destination doesn't turn out well, you've wasted the leverage of the trip. You've lost the process. You certainly, as a believer, have lost the chance to worship, to glorify God. You weren't worshipping the whole time. You were just fixated on the outcome, and when the outcome doesn't go your way, you lose the joy, you lose the peace.

Here's the problem with that. You lose the love for the game. *Why play it? We're not going to win anyways. Why keep playing? We're not going to win.* You can see that! It's so clear. Who is more motivated, the team that is way ahead or the team that is way behind? It's the team that has a winning record or the team who has a losing record. The team who's playing for the championship or the team that is just playing out its schedule, because the season's "over." It's not over! They may have most of the season left, but in their minds, it's "over." That's so incredibly de-motivating it's unbelievable. But when you have the wrong goal, and the wrong track, it's not going to end well.

Pursuing Winning as a Goal Inhibits Performance

The reality is, "winning" (as a goal) is demotivating when you get to certain places along the road. Now we're talking about psychology, about how bodies work emotionally and physically and mentally.

When you're way behind, the concept of winning is demotivating. When you're way ahead, it's demotivating because you've already "won" in your mind and so your level of play diminishes. Everybody knows it: that the majority response of a team that's way ahead in a contest is they lose their capacity to be completely focused on the mind, and in their emotions, which affects their body. Whether they're a Jesus person or not, these are just practical realities that everybody understands.

The game, once it gets out of hand, changes, unfortunately. This happens the vast majority of times, even for believers, because they don't understand this philosophy and the implications of what their power is, and what their target is. But if the goal is to glorify God, it doesn't matter if you're ahead or behind. It doesn't matter if you're playing or not playing. It doesn't matter if you've played poorly so far or played well because the next play is another opportunity. It doesn't matter if you're a manager or a trainer, a coach or a player, or a spectator. Glorifying God is always on the table.

The pursuit of winning as an outcome produces anxiety, tension, and fear of failure—not in everybody, but at some point along the path, this is part of the action. Take public speaking, for example. If you know you have to share in public, versus share in private, you feel something, whether you call it excitement, anxiety, or fear. In a similar way, the player who shoots the free-throw in the game-winning shot outcome has a different sensation in that moment than when it's the middle of the game or the start of the game or a game that doesn't "matter." He has a different feeling altogether in practice, and another when shooting hoops with friends in his driveway. It would be irrational to think otherwise. Everybody would acknowledge that these physiological, emotional, and mental factors are in play almost all the time, in any performance.

It has nothing to do with sport. Think about parenting. If you have to parent in front of somebody, versus parenting when nobody else is watching, you'll parent differently because you're thinking, or it crosses your mind, *I wonder what they think about how I discipline. Was I too hard? Was I too soft?* Head games, we call it. Psych outs. This is always in play. This is always in play when you're performing in a way that you're conscious of what other people are or might be thinking. Fear of man. Fear of failure. Fear.

Anxiety is fear. Concern is fear. It's just a lightened version of it. Anything that produces anxiety or tension or fear increases the chance that the body, emotion, and mind will be compromised from their optimum level of performance. And we've already said, the inside drives the outside. That the mind, emotions, and will shut down way before the body does. There's a direct correlation between the internal and external manifestations, in sports and life.

This isn't just about sport. Whatever you can do to disable those forces and causes so that you can play relaxed, so that you can play in the zone, so that you can play focused and uninhibited by circumstances, so you can become what we call "circumstance-proof," increases the chances that your outcome on a given play is better. That the gap closes between the performance and the potential.

"Winning," Play Time, and the Philosophy

I want to close out this chapter with some thoughts on how this philosophy of winning relates to playing time. **Playing time is a huge issue for players at all ages and experience levels.**

It's a huge issue for parents, obviously at the lower levels because parents are more involved. As players move up, they become less involved. But when they're little, parents are inevitably involved.

One of the jokes about doing youth sports, even up to high school, is the issues coaches have in dealing with parents. As primarily a college coach, I can only think of one example, so that's probably indicative of the dividing point that seems to happen between high school and college.

Of course, in youth sports, they have mandates that you put players in for some time. Once they get to junior high or high school, that may no longer be applicable, and a player may not play the whole year. What we're saying is, if you're a Jesus guy, and all you care about is outcomes, and the outcome is decided, why not give those players who don't play, an opportunity? Why wouldn't you? What does that feel like to a player?

I'm not saying we start players who are not competent. I have a responsibility as a coach to put the best team in the field that I can, for the sake of the institution. I can't have my agenda trump their agenda. If their agenda is to win, I need to strategize and coach in such a way to help them reach their goals. That's not in conflict with this philosophy.

Because even if our only goal is to win, this is the best philosophy—process over results. It's the best philosophy to maximize people physically, emotionally, mentally, and spiritually. It's the best philosophy for play even if you don't care about God and all you care about is winning, because it enhances people, enhances the process, and gets people to think to the next play or next day with wholeheartedness, without the inhibition of demotivating factors like continuously having before their face, "You must win, you have to win, you have to produce."

Of course, we all know you must produce. That's inherent. We're trying to maximize. Being aware that maximization doesn't always translate into playing time is a fabric of society. People get jobs and don't get jobs based on their productivity. We're not denying reality. We're just saying that reality is not going to be our motivator. We have a universal motivator with supernatural gas (Holy Spirit), supernatural instruction (the Word), and a supernatural and eternal endpoint.

The *Competing Biblically* philosophy works because it maximizes everything without limitations. Consider how a child feels when treated with disrespect or disinterest. Remember, every member is important. You have many parts but one team, and the weaker parts are indispensable.

Discussion Questions

1. How does redefining "winning" as glorifying God change the way we compete and coach in sports?
2. What does it practically look like to "aim for perfection" while still living under God's grace?
3. In what ways can pursuing outcomes, like winning, actually hinder performance and motivation?
4. How can we apply the "To-By-For" framework (TO the Word of God, BY the power of God, FOR the glory of God) outside of sports?

CHAPTER 11

GETTING THE BEST FROM YOUR INNER AND OUTER CIRCLES

*"The more one emphasizes winning,
the less he or she is able to concentrate on
what actually causes success."*
—Nick Saban

Success in sports—or any leadership endeavor—is never a solo act. It is born in community, shaped by relationships, and sustained by trust. As a coach, you're not just managing a team; you're stewarding a culture. Whether you realize it or not, you are surrounded by two powerful networks that can either fuel your mission or frustrate your progress: your *Inner Circle*—the staff and players who walk with you daily—and your *Outer Circle*—those whose influence may be quieter but no less vital: administrators, parents, fans, and friends.

We need to learn how to lead both circles with integrity, strategy, and Biblical wisdom. It's about building bridges, not silos. You're stepping into systems, expectations, and sometimes, the echoes of past leadership. But this is also your opportunity to bring clarity, foster unity, and model Christ-like service in every interaction.

To do this, you'll need to determine the key elements of your relationships with these circles and how to direct them effectively.

Building Bridges

How do you relate to those in the outer circle? In this case, we're going to talk about people you're serving, say the board or administration. If it's a school, there are responsibilities. Kids have to go to class even as they're playing sports. A big issue when working with outer-circle people, particularly in the first year, is bridge building.

These people have a preconceived notion of what your sport looks like and what it is. They have a notion based on their own story, what they've seen on TV or observed, and what they've seen at that school with previous coaches. You're coming into a situation where you can't control what the previous regime did or said, or whether they were a blessing or a curse. At some point, you have to dismantle stuff. You don't walk into a property and build on top of a bad foundation; you dismantle some and decide what you can build upon. This is all an evaluative process when you take over any sport, any team. At some level, unless you're the start of a new team or organization, you're inheriting something.

The first point is to get your outer circle to believe in you. If they don't believe in you or trust you or like you, it's going to hinder the process. They need to believe in the staff. Hiring, or whatever it is in your situation, is critical. Whom do you bring into the organization? Who's part of your team of leaders? What do people know about them and their history? This is a big deal.

Earn Their Buy-in

The second thing is to get your outer circle to believe in the vision and mission. Belief in the leaders from the outer circle is critical. They can believe in the leader yet not believe in the vision. Building this buy-in is essential. With the inner circle, your staff and your players, this is a no-brainer, but the outer circle needs buy-in too.

You can't control their perception or response. What you can do is pray that they're open. I've got friends in coaching right now who are having compromised experiences because the president of the organization they're serving either doesn't like them, doesn't support them, or is neutral. All of those situations are problematic. If they're neutral, it may not create resistance, but it doesn't assist because you need momentum. You need everybody on the same page.

We can use the example of rowing. If you have ten people in a rowboat, and nine people are rowing with all their hearts, and one person is not rowing, that boat will go slower. But if they stick their oars in the water, that creates resistance. You're going to be even slower than you would have been without them at all. It's amazing how much drag one person out of ten can create!

One scenario is that they're doing nothing, which diminishes your performance. The other is that they're passively resisting. The last is that they're actively resisting. This can happen from anyone. It can happen from your players. God willing it doesn't happen from your staff, and that you choose well. It can also come from parents of players; in youth sports parents are an incredible opportunity for momentum—but also can be a point of resistance.

Buy In to Them Too

Outer circle buy-in is more likely if the coach first shows belief in them. Don't go to a school where you don't buy into the larger vision, because your job is to implement it. Recognize that there's a dualism going on. You have your program but you're still working for a university or a city or a team. You're working for an entity bigger than your program, which is important to their view of you and your view of them. Hopefully, since the key people have hired you, in theory they already buy into you; you have to know this if you want to work for them. You need to know that you share the vision of the institution at some core level. Granted, you're not going to buy into everything, but you have to make a choice to buy into their goals, their vision.

Frankly, if you want God's will, God's will is that you be a blessing to the people you work for. When I come into an organization, I have the desire to implement their will, whatever it is. In that case, I'd better know what their will is so I feel positive about partnering with them.

For me, if I coach at a college, I want to be part of the process of higher education. If I don't care about education, if I don't care that kids go to class, that's not going to help. You're there to help them reach their goals. That's why when you go to an organization, and there's not a match between their goals and your goals, that's not sustainable. It increases the chance it's not going to go well from the start.

I will emphasize this: it's not about you. It's about God. It's about caring for others who are in the outer circle and considering them. The Bible says consider others better than yourself (Philippians 2:3–4). This needs to be part of the process of creating buy-in. I need to buy into the vision of the grander institution and give my whole heart, strong will, clear mind, and great passion to it. If we don't do this, how can we expect anyone else to do the same for our own vision?

You also need a holistic view of things, and do not simply think about sport in a vacuum. You also have to think about the students as if they're student-athletes, whether it's junior high, high school, or college. They go to school. You have to buy into the vision of the educational institution you either work for or supplement.

For example, in youth sports, we need to care—even though we don't work for a school—that the kids do their homework. Say you work for a parks and recreation department in your local community. I promise you the parks and recreation department doesn't want you focusing on outcomes on the scoreboard and not caring if kids do well in school. Parks and recreation are part of the city, which is also part of the school district, and there is crossover there that would be in your best interest to enhance.

I once worked for a university where athletes just got by as students. They didn't often go to class. I set a goal, and told the faculty and administration I was doing so, for every student athlete to attend every class. They laughed, because that hadn't been part of their culture. But my team and I were serious about it. We implemented repercussions for students who didn't meet that goal. Over the course of the three years we were there, we didn't completely reach the goal, but we made progress. The main thing was that we did the right thing, did it the right way, and stayed at it. Our efforts earned us the buy-in of the outer circle of that organization.

Be an Example for the Inner Circle

The inner circle is your other coaches, support personnel, and players. What's your relationship with the rest of the staff and the team?

Frosty Westering used to say, "I don't coach for a livin'; I coach for a lovin'." This goes back to a love of the game. Love God. Love people. This is much more important than you may realize. It's difficult to play, practice, prepare, pray, and commit to something you don't love at the highest level. If you're trying to give your whole heart, a clear mind, strong will, and great passion, but you don't like what you're working at, that's not going to go well.

We coach—or lead—for lovin', not for livin'. If you just want a paycheck, that's different than if you're energized by your job. And the motivation should be—even if it's something that's viewed as a menial job—"I'm here to glorify God." Work, in this way, is actually worship.

Earlier in this book, we talked about *sport* as worship. Work is also worship. When I work at that fast food restaurant, I am worshipping God. People are going to see Jesus by the way I handle the process. If you act like it's just a job, it's going to be hard for you to glorify God in the way you do the job. Again, the carryover of this philosophy is in all areas.

Players, support personnel, and players may only participate in your youth sport team for one year. But there they can learn, depending on how deeply you commit to communicating and how deeply they buy in. They can come away with lessons that translate into life.

Hiring Coaches in the Philosophy

The first point in Robert Coleman's *Master Plan of Evangelism* is selection. Jesus spent all night in prayer before He picked the twelve. It wouldn't have mattered what He did with the twelve if He'd picked poorly! We call this selection process in the *Competing Biblically* philosophy "FATC." Those disciples, though they were unschooled and ordinary men, were *faithful*, were *available*, were *teachable*, and were *courageous* to obey when there was risk. This is an example of the kind of player and coach you look for. This is our vetting mechanism of whom we want in our program. It's certainly whom we want as staff, or those we hire.

Frosty was always less concerned with people's competency than their heart. He said, "I can teach you how to coach but I can't teach you how to love." If you don't love the players, we've lost the mission, which is eternity. The mission and vision are tied with the target of eternity. We should be thinking about this in our own selection process. I care about how you coach, but I care less about that than how you love. This is part of the process of finding the people you're looking for.

When you recruit, sometimes you inherit teams, sometimes you get to choose—this is a big deal. But in either case you need to look at this principle. Even if you inherit your team, the bottom line is it's still a voluntary organization and you set the thermostat by establishing and communicating, "This is how we're going to do business here. This is how we're going to treat each other, coaches, the scoreboard, opponents, and officials." With eyes wide open, they can then voluntarily decide to be part of the organization. They can decide about continuing.

It's critical that they believe in you, that they believe in the staff—you need to make sure the staff are on the same page—because if the staff is not on the same page, they're going to communicate something different than what you're communicating. If there's dissonance, it's going to be problematic. It's like how children know when parents are at odds. Kids have no problem knowing that if Dad says no, they can go ask Mom. If Mom says yes, they've created tension in the marriage.

Our coaching staff has to be on the same page as us. If we're not on the same page, we've got compromised direction. We already are facing our own flesh and selfishness, not to mention the power of the culture and the powers of demonic forces that are trying to disable the mission. Glorifying God must be the mission and vision, for all of us. Even at a secular campus, I'm coaching in such a way that I glorify God, and we glorify God even if the players and parents don't care about God. We're still going to play and live in a certain way, biblically. Whether we can call it that or not, it's going to be biblical in orientation.

The whole staff needs to believe in the vision and mission. If they don't, you've got to graciously allow them out. If they say they do and they don't, that won't last. At every juncture, you've got to decide how seriously you deal with dissonance or lack of commitment from the inner circle.

Relationships within the Inner Circle

The players too need to be on the same page, need to believe in each other. The coaches need to believe in each other. There has to be trust. There has to be caring and sharing.

You don't wait for this to happen; you have to develop it. And, you have to have an intentional strategic plan to develop it. These things, for us, are more important than x's and o's. If you're competent in x's and o's and incompetent with relationships, you're going to hinder the chance of meeting your ultimate goal.

In your inner circle, there needs to be time spent together so you can build relationships. It's hard to build a relationship if you're never together. We have to work at that. We have to work at putting together people who aren't normally together.

When I go into a college as a consultant, and look at the teams, if the players are separate from the student body, that's a yellow flag. If the players are only meeting by their position groups, that's a problem too. If players are grouped up along racial or ethnic lines, that's another problem. If people who are older in the program are never with those who are younger in the program, that's an additional issue. It's not a deal-breaker, but it's a problem. We build synergy where players lay down their personal wants and take responsibility.

How do you change a program? If even one person disagrees, it can compromise the situation. While not everyone will always agree, aim for perfection and be dedicated to achieving it. This ensures your team has a better experience and fulfills the goal of glorifying God through evangelism and discipleship.

The Four Parts of Moving the Ball Forward

1. The Buy-In
2. The Rub
3. The Warning
4. The Cost (Death to Self)

The Buy-In

This means getting people on the same page. When I teach a class unrelated to sports, I need them to buy in. If they don't buy in, it's not going to enhance the experience. When you're in a classroom and someone's disinterested, you can tell. You can tell when people care and don't care. There has to be a buy-in by the people who are involved, the leaders. And then it helps to have the buy-in of those people they're serving.

The Rub

Selfishness is going to disable the process. Selflessness will enhance the process. We're not saying no self at all. We just want less self. More "we" than "me."

The Warning

This is when somebody may go sideways because something rubs them wrong. That's why we call it "the rub." It rubs them wrong, and they don't buy in, and then they passively or aggressively resist. Galatians 5:9 says, "A little leaven leavens the whole loaf." If somebody doesn't buy in, that resistance, whether passive or active, diminishes the chance that the program will get traction. It's no different in a spiritual sense. If this happens in a local church, if folks go there who don't participate, and leaders are presenting a vision and mission and people don't volunteer or engage, it doesn't gain any traction. If people grumble and complain in the background, it compromises. There's diminished spiritual power, and, practically speaking, it's going to disengage the process.

The Cost (Death to Self)

"The cost" refers to the target that coaches die to themselves for the players, and players die to themselves for the coaches. The target, in this ideal hypothetical world, is that the outer circle are supportive. In a sense, they die to their vision of what the team should look like and how they should play. They say, "We're going to be loyal, regardless of how we see and feel and think." Now, admittedly, that's flagrantly unrealistic. If you've been to a game where there's a lot of booing for the team you support, you know that doesn't enhance your experience. It's discouraging for people to voice their disapproval.

If you come to a school, you don't get to pick the coaches or the leadership. But you can make a decision about whether you want to participate or not. If you do choose to participate, you have a biblical responsibility to submit to the authority of the leadership there and have an attitude of "not my will but yours be done." That's incredibly difficult because of the warning, the rub, and the cost, for players and families and fans.

Inner Circle—Players' Perspective

This is their responsibility, and for us who are leading the charge, it's critical that we create a clear vision and implement it. Do the right thing the right way and stay at it. Here would be the issue of relationships with players, with each other, and with authority. It needs to be a total package, for the whole team:

#1. We versus Me—This is the whole issue of selfishness. It's got to be about we and not about me. It's not about me. It's about us. At every point there is going to be a rub with the flesh and a cost to die to yourself for the sake of the greater good. It's true in the Kingdom of God. It's true in any organization that wants to set the bar. There has to be a submission to each other. Scripture says submit to God and submit to one another (Ephesians 5:21). It's even true in marriage.

#2. Expectation—High expectations and high grace. There must be high expectations. If you have high expectations and low grace, you're going to have a dominating, oppressive scenario. If you have low expectations and high grace, you're never going to hit your target. There must be high expectations and high grace. With Jesus, the "high expectation" is obedience. The "high grace" is that, if you fail, you ask for and receive forgiveness—"Go and sin no more" (John 5:14, 8:11) Get back up and keep going. Get knocked down seven times, get up eight.

#3. Responsibility—As you walk further in an organization, whether it's the Kingdom of God or a family, you lose rights and gain responsibilities. There must be understanding. You don't gain all kinds of rights and lose responsibility. If you want to have more impact, you're going to gain responsibility and lose your rights. One of the fundamental rights you lose is the right to do what you want when you want it. It goes back to the famous John Wooden quote, "When you choose to become part of a team, you cease to exist as an individual." That's an example of lost rights and gained responsibilities.

#4. Discipline—This is the principle of order versus disorder, the principle of considering others as better than yourself. Exercise self-control. Discipline yourself so that others don't have to discipline you. It's a great line. The goal is to evolve to self-discipline, to order instead of disorder. When you come into an organization and attempt to implement this philosophy, you're going to have to create order, possibly, where there's currently disorder. There's going to be the introduction and practice and supervision of "we versus me," of articulating high expectations with grace, and of having the sense that responsibilities are going to be gained, and rights are going to be lost. And there's going to be order, discipline, and self-control as part of the process (i.e., "We'll teach you that until you choose it yourself.")

#5. Benefit—The benefit is that you're going to enjoy the trip. You're going to learn that it's better to serve than to be served. You're going to learn that giving is more fulfilling than receiving. You're going to learn the benefits of "me versus we." You're going to play better, and the experience is going to be enhanced because you're partnering with people and competing with them instead of competing against them.

How do you maximize your ability when you're against each other? A kingdom divided against itself will fail (Mark 3:24). And yet, when we create competition in a team, we create not a climate of blessing each other or being a blessing; instead, we introduce factors into the equation that diminish the process. It doesn't enhance relationships. It doesn't make the trip enjoyable. Somebody will rise to the top. He may have successful individual experience, but collectively, the experience will be compromised. The benefits are enjoying the trip, playing better, and seeing life impacts.

The Philosophy in Action

This "total package" is the coaching philosophy we are here to implement. If you choose to implement it, it will likely take three to five years, in our experience, to flip anything. If you're fortunate, and the mercy and grace of God are prevalent, and the factors you can't control are aligned, it might happen in two to three. The play on the field will be enhanced, but the extent is dependent on the talent of the people. If you don't have talented people, the culture can shift but the play may not, because at some point they have to become faster, stronger, and more experienced. There are things that take time to bake, unrelated to the culture.

If you're facing a situation where you encounter resistance within the inner circle or outer circle, it may take longer. Frankly, if that's the case, then they likely won't let you be in that position of leadership longer than that. There's a lot of impatience. There's a lot of the outer circle pushing for only what they want, which is often outcomes on the scoreboard.

You pray and you act. These two principles complement each other; we encourage you to err on the side of prayer. But there has to be action also. You pray and you act; you act and you pray. Repeat the process. Pound the philosophy verbally and visually, in every way you can conceive. Be consistent with articulation and supervision as much as possible. Do the right thing the right way and stay at it. You're at the mercy of God for the timing, the buy-in, every element. You can only do your part.

We close the gap between our performance and our potential. Players and overseers are also trying to close the gap. It's a very delicate situation in every way. Any one circumstance or person, inside or outside the circle, could blow it up, disable it, shut it down. And that's why we pray: God's will on Earth as it is in Heaven. If we do that, the right thing the right way and stay at it, as much as possible we're inviting God into the equation. We invite and allow the Holy Spirit, His power and fruit, to penetrate saved and unsaved people who have bought in a little or not at all. This is when the ball moves forward. And then you have the change.

Communicating the Values and Mission

The next and final point is about tangible ways to communicate the vision and mission of *Competing Biblically* within a program:

#1. See, Speak It, Hear It—We've discussed how critical it is to talk about the concepts of your philosophy, to put the ideals in the ears and mouths of your program. Make the principles visible; write them down where everyone can see them, and then add some more. Pound the philosophy into the eyes and ears with your confession. And get them to speak it aloud. This is what it means to be conscious of the principles of Deuteronomy 6.

We're always struck when people are interviewed, and they keep saying the company line. The company line is a repeat of what the organization's mission is. You'll hear them say it over and over. That's a learned response. It's learned because the overseer says it so much that eventually those under him or her repeat it. It's no different than a parent. How many of us as adults find ourselves saying things our parents said or doing things our parents did? We might not even have liked it, but we repeat it. What you see over and over, you tend to repeat. What you hear over and over, you tend to remember and articulate.

This is part of the reproduction process. If you see it or say it or hear it enough, it becomes you.

Now this can be either good or bad—that's a fact of how the human mind works. When you post things, when you speak about them, when you have people verbalize them, chances are greater that they are embraced. It's also true with the Word of God. If I look at the Word and read it, it affects my eyes. If I speak it, it affects my ears. The chances are greater it will stick if I involve more senses. What we're trying to do with this philosophy is speak it, hear it, see it, and use every opportunity possible to find a tangible way to communicate vision, values, and mission.

#2. Communicate Vision with Encouragement—Encouragement is part and parcel of this philosophy and of communicating and imparting it to your inner and outer circles. We want to use words to build up. An incredible way I've learned to do this through experience is writing people written notes. There's something powerful about a handwritten note. Touch is also powerful. It communicates genuine belief. We must work at using all the senses to articulate our principles.

"Put-ups" are words that raise somebody up. It's a paraphrase of Ephesians 4:29, "Let no unwholesome word come out of your mouth but only what will build others up." Some people consider it positive talk; we consider it more than that. "Good job" doesn't have as much impact as, "The way you ran for the ball in that play was great," or, "The way you finished the game with that attitude was good." The more specific you are, the more it's from your heart, the more chance it has of having impact than if it's just flippant words.

I'd rather hear "good job" than nothing, but I can say it in a different way that has more impact. That's a learned behavior. You can learn what you want to reproduce and what you don't want to reproduce from your mentors. God willing, we reproduce the things that we have experienced or have seen to have a powerful impact. When somebody is weeping and they look me in the eye and say thank you, they don't have to say much. Their emotions supercharge the words. They don't have to say anything. If there's emotion, if there's touch, there is a powerful impact.

Try this: write a note to every player on your team. Just a one-liner. Try to be specific. "It was fantastic to hear you cheer on the sidelines." Make sure that every other week, everybody receives at least one note. When we did this, at the end of the year when cleaning out lockers, we'd find all the notes saved by players. Not every guy, but regularly, there were notes taped in the lockers. For us, it took five seconds. To them, it meant something enough that they saved it, posted it, and reviewed it.

That's my epiphany of the power of words as a coach or as a parent. I could've said something, which may or may not have had an impact, but when it was written, there was something about it that had longevity that was different than words. Written letters are more meaningful than an email. When that letter or note has a "put-up" it's more meaningful. A "put-up" is just a blessing. You're blessing somebody by building them up.

In practice, what we would do to teach players to build others up, was say, "In this next ten-minute period, I want you to give three 'put-ups' to somebody on the team. At the end of ten minutes, we're going to debrief what it felt like to give the "put-up" and to receive 'put-ups.' We did that regularly. We would have 'put-up' sessions during practice. I was struck and the players were struck. They said it made them feel good. It connected them with someone else. "That guy said something meaningful to me, and now I feel closer to him." You're building intimacy. You teach them how to climb outside themselves, care about somebody else, and realize the power of words.

Everybody wins. That's how you create a culture of "put-ups." That's how you create cross-pollination, where people say something to someone outside their circle. Then you debrief. Now you've created a culture where people put each other up instead of nothing or putting down.

We learn about leveraging "put-ups" to enhance the experience, to build relationships horizontally, to draw people to Jesus vertically. It has a phenomenal impact, though it takes some time. You have to educate your players to make it authentic.

Reinforce the Afterglow

The afterglow is a post-game gathering, the after-a-contest time in which you bring the team and staff together to reflect and lift one another up. It started with Frosty Westering at Pacific Lutheran University. Frosty handled the post-game process better than anyone. You can do it with as much creativity and as wide or deep as you want.

Generally, teams gather together after a contest, whether on the court, the field, or in the locker room, and the coach makes some closing statements. In Frosty's case, what would later go on to be known as the Afterglow began with him sharing some thoughts with the inner circle, and then the players in the locker room immediately began to talk about the game and put each other up. Coaches put up players; players put up coaches. They'd spend half hour to an hour and half after the game doing this.

Eventually parents came, then family and friends, and they stayed with the team the entire team throughout the entire post-game process. After a while, the crowd compromised the experience of the inner circle, and the intimacy, so they decided to have two post-game sharing times. After every game, they'd have a private "put-up" session with the team and then they'd have a public Afterglow either in the locker room, the stands, or back on campus. It could be over an hour for the inner circle and then another hour or more for the public one, sometimes over three hours total, but no one was in a hurry to go. Granted, this was football, and it was generally happening in the afternoons. This time frame wouldn't likely work for everyone. You may only have 20 to 30 minutes; however, you can adapt the idea to your situation. The point is, what are you doing after the contest?

I remember, as a kid, going to Shakey's Pizza Parlor after games with families and teammates, and just being together. Those were great times. How much more impactful it would have been if the coaches had had some intentionality about blessing players and relaying encouragement for what happened during the game.

In the Afterglows I've participated in, the kinds of things that happened were powerful. People came to Jesus; many still have lifelong memories. It was often more powerful than the game itself! It could be about an interaction with a player, or a referee, or someone in the outer circle. Frosty's attitude was this: "If we're only together for eleven games a year for three or four years, for any individual player, let's enhance the experience by caring and sharing and enjoying the whole trip, game and post-game. Let's come out of this experience with value way beyond the game, certainly way beyond the scoreboard." This was the impact of the Afterglow.

Discussion Questions

1. *Inner vs. Outer Circle Dynamics:* How can a coach or leader intentionally build trust and alignment with both their inner circle (staff and players) and their outer circle (administrators, parents, community)? What challenges might arise in trying to balance the expectations of both circles?

2. *Buy-In and Vision Alignment:* We pointed out that "you need to buy into their goals, their vision" if you want others to buy into yours. How does this principle apply when coaching within a larger institution (school, church, city program)? What are some practical steps to identify and align with that vision?

3. *Addressing "The Rub" and Resistance:* In the "Four Parts of Moving the Ball Forward," we identified "The Rub" as a critical point where selfishness or resistance can derail momentum. How can a coach or leader discern early signs of resistance—whether passive or active—and how should they respond biblically?

4. *Selecting and Shaping the Inner Circle:* Reflecting on the "FATC" criteria (Faithful, Available, Teachable, Courageous), what qualities should you prioritize when building a coaching staff or recruiting players in a program that seeks to glorify God? How can love and unity be cultivated practically within the inner circle?

CHAPTER 12

BEING ON MISSION IN SPORTS

"Therefore go and make disciples of all nations, baptizing them
in the name of the Father and of the Son and of the Holy Spirit,
and teaching them to obey everything I have commanded you.
And surely I am with you always, to the very end of the age."
—Matthew 28:19–20

Jesus has called us to be "on mission" with Him. We call this the "Great Co-mission" (Matthew 28:16–20). What does it mean to be a "sports missionary"? We've talked a lot in this book about playing and coaching, but now we'll also talk about what it looks like as a spectator, parent, and administrator. What does this look like? What could it look like? What's the vision for it? We're going to discuss what a sports missionary is, what their role is, and what it means to go to the foreign country of sports.

Some people have compared the field of "sport" to a foreign country because it's like a culture. Sport in general is a culture, and each sport has its own culture—just like each country has its own unique culture, language, dress, food, and traditions. All of that is important to be aware of. If you want to do sports ministry, then you need to understand the language and culture of that sport, or you're going to be working against a language barrier.

Just look at the difference between how athletes and non-athletes think and talk. It's not a matter of wrong or right; it's just culture. Even the language and the metaphors they use are going to be different. Within sports culture, you will be using the language of sport.

Anybody who is on mission, who is living the Great Commission lifestyle, can be considered a "sports missionary." In their context, they're on a mission by God, according TO His Word, BY His power, FOR His glory, going into the mission field of sport.

The (Sports) Fields Are Ripe for Harvest

A missionary is one who is sent. I've heard that there are 40 million people on any given weekend in the United States who are having some interaction with sport—playing it, coaching it, watching it. Somehow, they're going to be affiliated. They say there are eight million high school athletes, male and female, in our country alone. Think about their parents and families and friends. That's a lot of people! Sport has a large audience in our country. Then there's the Super Bowl, and soccer's World Cup—the majority of the world is aware of what's going on during the World Cup. (The rest of the world has more of an infatuation with soccer than America does, but we're trying to catch up.)

These are examples of how countries and communities are driven by sports. There are jokes about how *Friday Night Lights*-type fever takes over whole small towns and everybody's at the sporting event. I live in Nebraska. On a Saturday afternoon, that stadium would be the third largest city in the state of Nebraska when it's filled with 100,000 people. This is the impact of sport.

When we talk about a sport missionary, we're talking about anyone who is sent on mission, the mission of God, to evangelize and disciple, to reach the lost and disciple the saved. This is the mission. We talk about being representatives or ambassadors. You are an ambassador for Christ. We're His representatives in everything we say and do.

Coaches can impact other coaches. Players and coaches can impact each other. I know stories of major universities where a player who was submitted to the Spirit of God was used in the salvation of a coach who saw this player play a different way. For example, we had a baseball player, Emeka Egbuka, on our Reality Sports faith-based competitive baseball team. He was a great baseball player but an even better football player. He was highly recruited as a receiver and signed to play at Ohio State University. He was part of a great gospel outreach on the Ohio State Campus where he and some other football players unashamedly shared their faith in Christ and baptized many at the event. It is reported that hundreds have come to Christ through his preaching and testimony.

Emeka was discipled in the "To-By-For" philosophy of competition and is displaying the Kingdom of God on his campus and will continue to be a sports missionary in the NFL. Sport, because of the power and influence and impact and passion associated with it, can produce incredible testimonies and examples if we simply live and play "To-By-For."

With that in mind, let's visit several roles in the context of sport, specifically outer circle roles, and what they can look like as sport missionaries.

The Role of the Parent

What is the role of a parent who is a sport missionary, whose desire is to adopt and emulate this philosophy? He or she is going to need to be educated in the philosophy, and that can happen in a number of ways. (There are different ways people learn.)

Now, it may be that a parent goes to a sporting event where they get a chance to observe this philosophy and they ask, "Why did they do that?" Whether they observe it first and then get information or whether they get information and then observe it, at some point in the sequence there must be an explanation of the process.

Odds are they're not going to understand the concept of competing biblically before they've heard about it, because they wouldn't necessarily know what it looks like. If they did, they might articulate it incorrectly, thinking that to be a godly person in sports is simply to be not as competitive. The world would say that to be a Christian athlete or coach is to just play for fun instead of with a competitive spirit. The truth, however, is that those who are filled with the Spirit of God, who are playing BY His power, FOR His glory, according TO His Word, should be the most focused, the most intense. They should be most competent in closing the gap between their potential and their performance, because the Spirit of God is energizing them.

So, for a parent who wants to embrace this, they are not playing at this point; they could be a coach or a volunteer, but let's say they're a spectator—the four stages of learning will apply at some point. They are going to hear or see, under your coaching, the concept of competing biblically. And frankly, a parent, though they're not playing competitively, will be given the opportunity to emulate this philosophy as a spectator of the sport their son or daughter is playing in. They're going to hear it and see it. They're going to practice it themselves at some level. At some point, they may even teach it themselves. It could be to another parent. It may be within the sport context. In a sense then, they're going to be the communicators of the philosophy. They can be an encouragement. They too can build up others with their words.

Parents can model the philosophy in the outer circle; they can spectate according TO the Word of God, meaning they are biblical in what they do, BY the power of God, relying on His power and not their flesh or selfishness for their child's favor. Of course they want their children's best, but they need to want God's will more. This is the point.

Do you want God's will or your will? Are you willing to say, "Not my will but Yours be done"? Luke 14:26 says, "If anyone comes to me and does not hate father and mother, wife and children, brothers and sisters—yes, even their own life—such a person cannot be my disciple." Was Jesus trying to say that we should hate those people who are dearest to us? No. But compared to the love for God and His will, it's as if we hate those people who are dearest to us in the flesh. If we're not willing to say that, if we're not willing to love God like that in comparison to our most intimate relationships, then perhaps we don't understand the Scriptures and the commitment and the cost that's involved.

If I want my child's best, even if it means God is not glorified, that would be problematic. If I want my child's best, even if it means disobeying the Scriptures, that would be problematic. If I want my will for my child and that team over God's will, that would be problematic. And yet this is the crux of exposing our hearts.

Think about the conversation you have with your child post practice: is it to build them up? There are horror stories of kids driving home with their parents who are criticizing them, even when they're young. There are all kinds of stories of parents who, for unbiblical reasons, are demoralizing, diminishing, criticizing, injuring, hurting, or scarring their own family, even as they confess Jesus. In the name of what? Certainly not in the name of God. Certainly not To-By-For.

This scenario is not an abnormal exception. This is a regular occurrence. All you have to do is attend a youth sport. It's a standing joke, to the shame of the body of Christ, that Christians fall prey to the same forces that unbelievers do in how they approach a sporting event as spectators. When we act to glorify ourselves or our team, we lose the opportunity to impact the Kingdom through the sport. When we go home and grumble and blame others, we injure our kids and disable our own walk. Yet we feel we have some right to do that because we want to win. We make idols of sport, of winning, and even of our own children.

Instead, we propose that we use parent-child sport programs as opportunities where parent and child can engage in the sports and work in a relationship that turns out to be discipleship. The parent partners with the coach in that context to show the child how to respond to coaches, officials, authority figures, and the opponent. The child learns how to use sports to glorify God instead of sports using us to glorify ourselves or the devil.

One slight exception to this is when a parent is officially coaching their own kid. What does that look like? As a guy who has coached his own children, I admit there's a tension there. There's a responsibility as a coach that is different than a responsibility as a parent. We encourage parents to be respectful and supportive of coaches and authority figures and be a blessing to their children for giving it their best shot, regardless of the outcome.

When you're in the role of coach, you wear two hats, and it gets tricky. It's hard for the kids sometimes because they wonder, *Is that my dad talking to me or my coach talking to me?* Depending on their psychological makeup and a variety of things, you may, with a good heart, intend to do one thing and it gets misunderstood and turns out to be another thing—and it becomes uncomfortable or painful. It's tricky when you're wearing two hats. It's not impossible; it can even be a great opportunity. But you need to be "wise as a serpent and gentle as a dove" (Matthew 20:16). It can be helpful in this situation to involve people from the outside to observe the way you communicate with your child, and give you honest feedback.

No matter how mature you think you are it can be difficult to see from up close whether your child is responding well to their parent who is coaching them, and to ensure that God is glorified and the relationship is enhanced rather than compromised. I've heard many disappointing stories along that line, where parents who are coaches give too much favor to their child or are too hard on their child, both of which are problematic. There are so many ways it can go sideways.

This is why it's important to be wise and discerning and to invite outsiders to observe. The dynamic is complicated and can leak from the field into the car and into the home. It can make or break your child's relationship to sport, and to you.

The Role of the Coach

It is good to ask questions and reflect on why we compete and coach the way we do. We have asked ourselves these questions for years and want to pass them down to you:

1. Are we aware of the impact we have within sport?
2. Are we aware of how much sports impact a culture?
3. Are we looking for opportunities for advancing life education?
4. Are we aware of the lifestyle evangelism and discipleship opportunities that competing biblically provides?
5. For whom do we play or coach?
6. Are we known as servant leaders?
7. Are we aware of the impact coaches have within sport?

As we begin answering these questions, it takes us into what one of my old coaches used to call "soul searching." I remember sometimes after practice he would bring us together and say, "Some of you guys need to go home and do some soul searching. What do you really want out of this game? Are you doing all you can to accomplish your goals?" He must have been seeing guys going through the motions or maybe he was just trying to teach us a life skill. His talks must have worked, though, because, 35 years later, I still remember the "soul searching" process.

I believe it is crucial to review these questions regularly. If you are reading this book, I am preaching to the proverbial choir and you already know this to be true. However, let's review and do some more digging into our souls and allow the truth of God's intention and purpose to saturate our thinking.

> *"A good coach can change a game;*
> *a great coach can change a life."*
> *—John Wooden*

"The greatest coaches aren't just game changers,
they are life changers."
—Tony Dungy

"A great coach can lead you to places
you never thought you could reach."
—Pat Summit

"A coach's job is not to make decisions for the players
but to guide and equip them to make
the right decisions themselves."
—Greg Glassman

Who we are and what we believe is significantly a result of the influence of others. It is our parents, mentors, disciplers, and coaches (which could be all of the above). As I write this book, it is 2025 and close to 2,000 years since Christ walked the planet. Here we are today as a result of Jesus and the 12 disciples reproducing and multiplying to the ends of the earth. We are thousands of miles away from Jerusalem and still talking about Jesus of Nazareth because of a vested few who reproduced and multiplied. That is fascinating to us. (This is the "Master Plan" of evangelism and discipleship, but more on that soon.) It is His one and only plan. He knew it would succeed even through what appeared to be a group of ordinary men.

It is also the plan we are attempting to implement through sport, a proven method from the Master himself. The power of a coach/mentor using intentional methods cannot be underestimated. The impact you have within sport is monumental.

Think again about how sport has captured a large segment of the population. Worldwide, think about how many people in a week observe a sporting event through TV, podcasts, in person. I just left Phoenix, Arizona, where hundreds of thousands of people will be headed in a few days to watch Major League Baseball Spring Training. Other cultures are even more ferocious than Americans in their thirst for soccer/*futbol*. Are we aware of that impact? Are we thinking about it in terms of the ramifications we have as players and coaches? God can use that and wants to use that—and will use that—if we but partner with Him in the process of sports.

Whatever it is that qualifies as sport: are we leveraging that? Dr. Robert Coleman, author of *The Master Plan of Evangelism,* would say, "Why would anyone play a round of golf if it wouldn't be to advance the Kingdom? Take someone with you to golf and use it to minister." Some people would say this is being too intense over this issue. Well, all we know is that people are dying, physically and spiritually. Once they're dead physically, if they haven't had a born-again experience, they will be separated from God forever. It's a pretty serious matter! At the same time, sport was meant to be enjoyed. The trip was meant to be enjoyed with pleasure, satisfaction, and redemptive capacity.

So, even as we're talking about advancing the Kingdom, that doesn't diminish how refreshing and fulfilling sport can be. It's not one or the other. Some of the most intense environments I've been in, as a player and coach, were incredibly fun in the process of that kind of intensity: the pleasure of enjoying the sport, enjoying the game, enjoying the competition, enjoying teammates, and enjoying the battle. Frosty Westering always said, "Enjoy the trip!" This is about realizing the opportunities we all have as coaches to advance the Kingdom. Let's have some fun enjoying the process!

The Impact of Sports on Culture

Sport not only impacts individual lives but the culture as well. A few years ago, when the Seattle Seahawks won a Super Bowl and went on to another, the city was electric. I attended the Super Bowl parade to cheer on the team—along with 1,000,000 other people! The impact their winning had on the culture of Seattle and the entire Pacific Northwest was incredible.

I've never been to Europe, but I have heard about the cities with teams in the Premier League. Their fan base and support is famous worldwide and it's definitely on my bucket-list to witness it in person.

We might ask, "How useful can these events be in advancing the Kingdom?" The answer is . . . VERY! Think of the Kingdom opportunities that arise with block parties, playoff gatherings, or attending a kids' volleyball match. What about coaching a youth sports team because the town is crazy for baseball, soccer . . . whatever? If you don't want to coach, you could work in the concession stand, or volunteer to get the field prepped and mowed.

In the town I live in, there is a local sports ministry camp with an attendance of 600 kids. There are 150 volunteers who work there and support the camp. Those kids hear the gospel, and bring their parents to the end-of-week Friday night service and camp celebration. That sports camp has a huge impact on that community/culture.

Another way culture can be impacted by sports is by the game-time event itself. I have been around Christian high schools and Christian colleges where two Christian schools played each other in a contest. I've seen some of those games display no visual sign of Kingdom-advancing impact. In fact, I have witnessed total embarrassment of the way the Kingdom was dishonored at some of those events (see Chapter 1). The negative impact on culture was displayed on full volume, with the advancement of self, selfishness, personal pleasure, and ego on full display.

However, I have also seen contests played by schools where the Kingdom was 100 percent advanced by strategic coaches. Jesus was glorified through both the winner and the loser. Both teams prayed together after the game, honored the officials, and honored the fans. That is a beautiful sight to behold when the impact is evident in the lives of all in attendance.

Once you've seen the power of how sport can be used to advance the Kingdom and transform lives, you will never go back to the world's system.

Opportunities for Advancing Life Education

We have to remind each other as coaches to stop practice when we have an opportunity to advance life education. I'm not only talking about spiritual stuff (although it is all spiritual stuff!). I'm talking about principles that will help people to be better friends, students, husbands, wives, fathers, mothers, neighbors, and workers. Take time to use the sport to develop people in terms of civil society and life education: caring, sharing, sacrifice, serving, and leadership. All of these things are on the table.

We've had coaches say when we teach this, "If I stopped every time there was an educational moment, we'd never practice!" Fair point. We believe being competent as a coach is important and getting reps at practice is mandatory. We are simply saying that you can make an impact by recognizing key moments in a practice when something was said or done that could be used as a life-educating moment for the team. At the minimum, we would suggest using a post-game practice talk to recognize some of the good things you saw from a character-building standpoint.

Become a coach who hones your craft in emphasizing the life-building skills a practice provides. Sport is about education, life education, and eternal education. It is about creating a vision for the lives of our athletes. Most of the kids we have coached are high school and college athletes, roughly 14–22. We talk about a 50-year impact with them. We talk about preparing them for their future impact on their generation and generations to come. We are not just talking about this season or next season, but the next 50 years. It's not just about this team but about legacy. It's about the generations. It's not even about us. It's about our children and our children's children. This, to us, is biblical thinking.

Opportunities for Lifestyle Evangelism and Biblical Discipleship

As stated earlier in this book, we are called as believers to evangelize and disciple. There are two types of people on the planet and on our teams. They are either lost or saved. There are two types of fans in the stands: lost or saved. There are two types of officials/umpires on the field: lost or saved. There are two types of athletes and coaches that are our opponents: lost or saved. If we see these individuals through the lens of the Great Commission, it hopefully makes us pause and come up with a plan to fulfill the Great Commission using sport.

Imagine if we could look at the entity of sport as a country and we were called to this country as missionaries. We would travel to this country called Sport and arrive with one thing in mind: to display the Kingdom of Jesus through our play and actions. The opposing team are the local natives from the country as we give them our best effort in our play with excellence and competence. We would have already worked at preparing to the best of our ability our play and strategy to honor them with the best skill and talent we could provide and give them a competitive game. The fans are from the local village as well, cheering on the contest between their hometown heroes and us, the visiting missionaries.

The officials/umpires are the ambassadors of the country we call Sport. Their job is to keep everything in order and officiate a fair contest. Every missionary will tell you the importance of honoring and serving the people of the country to which they have been called. Their hope is to display the love of Christ and reach the country for which they have prayed and trained.

Wouldn't it be crazy if the missionaries showed up to the country of Sport and ripped the ambassadors of the country when calls went against them? Wouldn't it be crazy if we showed up as missionaries and taunted the local village people we were trying to reach? Wouldn't it be crazy if the local village people in the stands were harassing us from the stands and we harassed back at them?

I know it may sound like a silly comparison, but this is the way we want to look at the competition day, and the power of lifestyle evangelism that sports provide. We really do believe that we are sports missionaries trying to display the Kingdom of God in everything we do.

Scotty once asked me if I wanted to see the other team come to Christ more than I wanted to win. I would like to say that, of course, I wanted their salvation more. However, at that particular time in my life, there was still a lot of "I want to win AND see them come to Christ." Truth be told, I had never really considered praying for the other team to come to Christ by the way I played and coached!

The platform sports provides for lifestyle evangelism is incredible. Do we realize this and really believe it?

When you buy into the Competing Biblically philosophy and begin to implement it into your team, the discipleship opportunities are abundant. Discipleship will usually be with your own players and coaches as relationships are built over time. The games themselves, which we call "live bullets," are great teaching moments and live laboratories of implementing To-By-For.

I know of a school, Scottsdale Christian Academy, in Scottsdale, Arizona, that has implemented the discipleship process of competing biblically. Their athletic director and coaches consistently meet and encourage each other in coaching according TO His Word, BY His power, and FOR His glory. They have strategic and intentional times with their athletes where they teach them how to walk in the power of competing for the glory of God.

Over the years, we have had the opportunity to disciple many coaches in the philosophy through prayer and Bible study. We realize that not everyone buys into the philosophy. However, for those who are FATC (Faithful, Available, Teachable, and Courageous), it is life-transforming. As we continue on the path of discipleship, we believe the evangelism will explode through the athletes and coaches.

Remember Whom You're Serving

Do we do it for ourselves or others? Is this about us and our fulfillment? Is it about me or others? Is it about the future or about now?

Long-term impact is correlated to how we view sport for our gratification or for others' edification. This is really important to consider. It is a natural thing to say, "I just want to play. I just want to go to games and enjoy myself." That is fine in natural thinking, but the problem is that, when we signed up with Jesus, we said, "Not my will, but Yours be done."

It's not your life. It's not your fun. It's not your comfort. It's about Him. If you want to do true Christianity, you're crucified with Christ. You no longer live, the Scriptures say (Galatians 2:20). Even in the sport context, Coach John Wooden said, "When you choose to be part of a team, you cease to exist as an individual." When you choose to become part of the family of God, you die to yourself.

This is the agreement and covenant we signed. Unfortunately, the gospel isn't always presented that way. Playing and coaching aren't always presented that way. When we surrender and coach for a higher calling, we fulfill the Great Commission through sport. The cool thing is that when you die to yourself, you actually live. In theology, we call this "The Great Exchange": your stinky, old, dead self in exchange for the riches and glory of Christ.

In coaching and playing, we need to have another type of great exchange: your desires and wants as a player and coach—which, by the way, are rooted in selfishness and pride, as well as great deception in trying to fulfill and find something that doesn't exist (just ask Adam). Let's exchange our will for His will in our coaching and play. We just don't become the best version of ourselves; we literally become His version—Jesus playing and coaching through us by the power of the Holy Spirit. You play and coach with supernatural freedom. It truly will become for the glory of God.

Coaches as Servant Leaders

There are various trains of thought on servant leaders today and the phrase is thrown around a lot in business and sports culture. If we want to look at servant leadership, we need look no further than Philippians 2, where the Apostle Paul talks about Jesus leaving Heaven as a King to come to Planet Earth and give His life for a fallen human race. He came not to be served but to serve and to give His life as a ransom for many. That's why He came. He did not come to relax and have fun with the disciples. He came with purpose and intentionality, modeling servant leadership. He asks us to follow Him and do likewise. He gives us the power and capacity to fulfill the calling through the power of the Holy Spirit.

Sport is a way to have these conversations about true servant leadership. The servant leadership model we want to exemplify is about heart transformation and not behavior modification.

Scotty had the unique experience of coaching two different teams, each led by head coaches who emphasized servant leadership in contrasting ways. One coach enforced discipline through consequences such as running laps or doing pushups whenever the dugout wasn't cleaned after practice or games. While he regularly spoke about servant leadership, his methods leaned more toward a "have-to" mentality rather than fostering a genuine desire in the players to serve. Scotty didn't necessarily believe the coach was wrong for instilling discipline in this way, but it didn't align with the deeper philosophy of heart-driven servant leadership that he valued.

The other coach Scotty worked with also preached servant leadership, but with a distinct focus on the privilege and responsibility of serving others. He would often remind players that cleaning the dugout was not just a task—it was a way of honoring those who would use the space after them. He framed it as a matter of respect and character, emphasizing that how the team left the dugout said something about who they were.

One game day, both head coaches happened to be absent. Scotty observed a telling difference in the players' behaviors. The team coached by the discipline-heavy leader neglected to clean the dugout, seemingly because there was no one there to hold them accountable. In contrast, the team led by the coach who emphasized heart transformation cleaned the dugout without being prompted. Scotty even overheard players quoting their absent coach's guiding principle: "Leave it cleaner than you found it."

We believe this is the target within servant leadership. We want the heart that wants to serve, the heart that has been transformed by the power of serving. We love others because He first loved us. Likewise, we serve others because He first served us.

Spectators as Missionaries

Spectators, as well as players, have a responsibility to act according to "To-By-For." Some fans and spectators are even more passionate than players, and it's a fine line between fandom and worship. Many do not even realize they have fallen into idolatry. In my experience, it may be harder for Christians to see the applicability of being a "To-By-For" biblical spectator because they see the philosophy as applying to the players and coaches and not to the fans. Our recommendation is that we all, inner circle and outer circle alike, have a conviction to be missionaries. Play on mission. Coach on mission. Spectate on mission. How you handle observing a sporting event has an impact on others.

The spectator may not know anybody on the team. They know their names, possibly, but don't have a personal relationship. In a sense, they're detached from it, and it's almost as if they feel they have a right to emulate traits that we would easily flag as problematic when seen through the lens spectating biblically—but they aren't thinking critically. If you fall in love with something or someone, to whatever degree you fall in love, your critical thinking decreases to that same degree. People focus on that object of love—in this case sport—to the exclusion of all else. People are crazy about their teams.

When something grabs you, and your affections are more for that than Christ, that's idolatry. That's what it called anytime you worship something more than God.

Your second priority in life should not even be remotely close in the standings. And yet people are casual in their relationship with God and fervently passionate about their team. This is the dark side of the power of sport. What we're trying to do is we're trying to take sport, which is neutral, from the dark side to the light side. To use it instead of sport using us.

There's no question that sport has been used to divide people, normal people who are functioning fine—but when it comes to sport, their team, their child, they lose it. I've been in it; I understand. I'm watching a TV game of a team I love, and someone wants to spend time with me, but I don't want them around. I want to watch the game. That can be problematic. None of this is to say I'm for abstinence from sport fandom. I merely advise we all consider if sport may have a hold on our hearts more than would be wise. Consider that our fandom may hinder the Kingdom, based on how we approach it.

Ephesians 4:29 says, "Do not let any unwholesome talk come out of your mouth, but only what is helpful for building others up according to their needs." Think about how we talk about our players and our opponents. We ought to have helpful, encouraging words to say about players on another team—no matter how selfish, arrogant, or proud they may be. The behavior of others doesn't give us a right, biblically, to speak ill of them or to want them to be injured or humiliated. This is not from the Spirit of God—not because they're good guys, not because they care, but because we're biblically bound to commandments and principles that should direct our attitude.

Sadly, when athletes perform poorly, many feel entitled to speak harshly about them: "I hope he gets cut. I hope he loses his job. I hope we trade him." But this attitude does not advance the Kingdom. It's unbiblical to think that sports somehow exempt us from Scripture. We can't ignore verses like Ephesians 4:29 just because a game is on. Our words have weight—they can grieve the Holy Spirit. When we speak in ways that don't build others up, we not only harm them but also those who hear us.

Scripture is clear: "Get rid of all bitterness, rage, and anger" (Ephesians 4:31–32). Yet, even godly men who confess Jesus as Savior can step onto the field or court and act in ways that contradict their faith. The Bible calls us to put that kind of behavior to death. Still, sports often become a space where we feel justified in saying or doing things we wouldn't elsewhere.

But when God said, "And whatever you do, whether in word or deed, do it all in the name of the Lord Jesus" (Colossians 3:17), He meant exactly that—no matter the context.

A Warning to Coaches

I know Christian coaches who have become the punchline among nonbelievers—examples of the hypocrisy they see in Jesus-confessing leaders. Whether it's their attitude, language, unethical hiring practices, treatment of women, or moral failures, these behaviors stand in stark contrast to the faith they profess. I've been on teams with coaches who claim to follow Christ yet disregard Scripture in the way they talk about other coaches, teams, or schools.

I'm not claiming innocence—I'm sure I've fallen into the same trap at times. But the real question is: do I want to obey? Too often, this behavior is excused with, "Well, in the heat of battle, things happen." But true repentance doesn't make excuses. True repentance grieves over sin.

If we can't recognize that this kind of speech is unwholesome— meant to tear down rather than build up—then we've misunderstood what Scripture calls us to.

As a fan, coach, or player, we need to think about those who oppose us, and use the line Frosty uses, "They came to beat us, we came to be us." When somebody comes to beat you and humiliate you, it's only by the Spirit of God that you can love and bless them. These are the kinds of rubs that we find in this philosophy practically.

Coaches set the tone. Coaches create the culture. As leaders, our attitudes set the example for our coaching staff and players. As we see in Old Testament examples in the Scriptures, when we're complaining about our circumstances, we're complaining about our Maker, who is Sovereign over our circumstances. When we grumble and complain about our boss (or our coach, the ref, etc.), we teach our children to complain about their authority figures. We model it, even if we don't have conviction about it. We think we have a right to use certain words and attitudes toward others because they have offended our child or our team. In essence, we are saying, "You offended my idol. And when you offend my idol, I react."

My idol could be the Seahawks or my son or my city or my country. When you touch my affection, and the affection of God isn't infinitely more powerful than that, then you smoke something out in my soul, my mind, or my emotions that is not going to glorify God. And that is why we are committed to the transformational impact of this philosophy—every language, every culture, every nation, every time, until He returns.

The Local Church and the Sports Mission Field

Now let's talk about the role of the local church in biblical competition and the sports mission field. This is a powerful opportunity.

Certainly, in our country, the cultural environment has become increasingly a club sport atmosphere for youth sports. People feel pressure to pay lots of money; if they don't, they feel like they are not giving their kids a chance. Families who are passionate about sport are being funneled aggressively to elite teams that play year-round. Kids are playing fewer varieties of sports because they're concentrating at an earlier age at a specific sport. Most of this is because parents want their kids to earn a college scholarship, or become pro-athletes.

We embrace an approach where people play multiple sports as long as they can. This is not a right or wrong thing. This is not a sin issue. There is, however, the risk of falling to idolatry. The constant pervasive practice and play can end up stealing from the family or local church.

Most of these club sports have weekend tournaments. What's the impact on the local church? For parents and children who are involved in the club sport, their relationship with the local church is compromised. This can cause angst for pastoral staff, for parents who feel guilty, and for the kids. This trend has compromised the Body of Christ.

I think there's another way to consider this, however. That would be to see families—parents and kids both—as being sport missionaries during times when being with their church community on Sunday is no longer possible. We're encouraging churches to adopt this thinking of youth athletes and parent spectators as missionaries. The bottom line is, if there are 40 million people who are involved in sports on a given weekend, many of them are not going to be able to go to church. They will be on the field or the court. Many of those people will be unbelievers.

Some believers will deal with conviction because they think they should be at church but they're not. Some, however, will be able to use the sport. Those who treat sport in this way are rare, because frankly, the Church hasn't embraced it. Most local churches merely tolerate sport or have ill will toward it because it has taken away people who are part of the fabric of their community. Every football season I lose regularity with church, as others do during tournament seasons. That's the playing field, so to speak, that we're on. Our contention is that rather than fighting it, we use this situation.

This is an opportunity where the Lord is showing us to the mission field of sport, which unbelievers are at every weekend in droves. Why not, rather than see it as a negative, see it as a positive? Why not see it as an opportunity to infiltrate the sport community, which is largely unsaved, not unlike the world? The Scriptures say the harvest is plentiful; the laborers are few. It's a massive mission field that a Jesus-confessing person could be infiltrating with the love of God. And it's as simple as being in a relationship with these people who might otherwise never set foot in the local church.

Why not think of the families absent on Sundays as missionaries? How about training them in how to present the gospel? How about training them in building relationships that move people forward in conversation about Jesus or salvation or discipleship? How about seeing them as the hands and feet of Jesus that we send out, rather than grudgingly miss? We send them out intentionally, with purpose. We send them out strategically, with a plan for them advancing the Kingdom in the sport fields of the country. I see this as a commission from God.

These all-day or sometimes multi-day tournaments have so much dead time where there could be conversation. There could be meals, there could be fellowship, there could be driving together. There's lots of time spent together in the sports context, particularly on the weekends when these people can't go to the local church. We should be using this time to glorify the Lord, and the Church should be enabling it.

Bring the sports families in front of the church, lay hands on them, anoint them with oil, pray for them, and bless them and send them off. Encourage our kids to think about evangelizing and discipleship in the context of their play.

On this mission field, in these playing fields of America, we've already got people in place. How about we give them a vision for evangelism and discipleship? How about we embrace it instead of disdain it? It is past time the Church had a plan to use sport to advance the Kingdom. We need to make sure it's a good plan and we execute the plan.

We have common ground with the lost through sports, and sports bring us into a relationship with them. It may be the only connection we have with them. Frankly, if it weren't for our kid playing on the same team, we wouldn't even know them, let alone spend time with them. And now not only do we know them, but we spend more time with them than other people in our circles by far. Who else do we see a night or two a week, and a day or two each weekend, for hours at a time? How about we see that as an asset instead of a liability? This is what we propose. Use sports, travel sports, and youth sports, to advance the Kingdom. Go where they are instead of asking them to come to us, to do the works of the Kingdom outside of the church walls as well as inside.

Discussion Questions

1. *Impact of Sports on Culture:* How can sports events and teams serve as platforms for advancing the Kingdom of God? Reflect on how a major local sports event, like a Super Bowl win or a local youth camp, can impact the surrounding community both spiritually and culturally.

2. *Opportunities for Life Education:* How can coaches use sports practices as a tool for life education beyond just athletic skills? Share examples of moments when sports provided a unique opportunity to teach important life lessons such as leadership, sacrifice, or teamwork.

3. *Lifestyle Evangelism through Sports:* How can coaches and athletes view themselves as missionaries within the context of sports? Discuss how adopting a "To-By-For" mindset can influence the way you compete, coach, or even spectate at a game.

4. *Coaches as Servant Leaders:* Reflect on the difference between behavior modification and heart transformation in coaching. How can coaches embody true servant leadership that fosters a spirit of voluntary service and character development in athletes?

CHAPTER 13

THE FIELDS ARE RIPE FOR HARVEST

"I tell you, open your eyes and look at the
fields! They are ripe for harvest."
—John 4:35

"Day after day, in the temple courts and from house
to house, they never stopped teaching and proclaim-
ing the good news that Jesus is the Messiah."
—Acts 5:42

Most of us don't coach or play in a specifically Christian climate, where the fullest expression of the To-By-For philosophy can be used openly. The majority of programs, schools, and teams in our country are secular. Many public-school sports programs aren't just unwelcoming to the philosophy but may be outright hostile toward anything of a spiritual nature. So, if you want to implement To-By-For in a secular program, then you'll have to frame it differently, either a lot or a little, depending on what part of the country you're in, who is running the league, etc. What you can contribute—as far as bringing a biblical worldview or content goes—is going to vary state by state, even community by community. That's why, when we talk about teams, we say each one is on some level a unique "country."

Coaching Biblically in a Secular Setting

There are certain things that are normative for how a particular sport is played, but the climate and the culture may be completely different between programs. Even if you have the approval of everyone within the program, the prevalence of social media means that anything can end up being overheard or seen by people who want to disdain, shame, or destroy the witness of the testimony of Jesus. The cultural landscape has shifted. That fact is not something people disagree with.

So, that being the case, how does a coach or an administrator at a secular organization walk out To-By-For? What does that look like? If this is the situation you find yourself in, it is essential to be wise as a serpent and gentle as a dove, because you're navigating delicate territory. This is just talking about the mundane opposition, to say nothing of the spiritual forces involved.

If you don't first address the spiritual world through prayer, you may have difficulty gaining traction, no matter how many worldly factors seem to be on your side. Even at a school where spirituality is welcomed, you could have spiritual warfare issues that may be obstructing the philosophy to take root. Remember that "our struggle is not against flesh and blood, but against the rulers, against the authorities, against the powers of this dark world and against the spiritual forces of evil in the heavenly realms" (Ephesians 6:12). There are forces that don't want Jesus to be glorified and His name lifted up.

At the personal level, one of the most critical keys to succeeding in a secular environment is going to be watching your words. Sadly, you can't use the name of Jesus in certain settings. You can't spell out your intent to lead To-By-For. Despite these things, you are not shackled from praying aggressively. Nobody can stop you from praying silently for or about the schools or public institutions. God is not blocked. The Kingdom is advancing.

You may need to be wise and creative, but we have found that this philosophy can succeed in secular settings also. If the gospel is unhindered in the heart of Hindu territory and Buddhist territory, God is certainly not blocked by some school system or policy. I trust you understand that everything is under His feet. We are His ambassadors, and everything is under our feet also—through the Word of God and prayer.

The Ten Commandments, Hold the Religion

One way I have found to successfully lead To-By-For in a secular environment is to learn how to distill biblical teachings to their value statements and present them without any of the religious context. For example, here is an articulation of the Ten Commandments that won't set off any secular alarm bells:

1. Respect and honor authority figures.
2. Watch your language.
3. Take time to rest and refresh.
4. Honor your parents.
5. Be kind and considerate to one another.
6. Respect one another's relationships.
7. Respect one another's possessions.
8. Be honest.
9. Be content with what you have.
10. Respect and honor people who have different beliefs.

Does that sound like something offensive? Even if I were an unbeliever, I would be encouraged if my son or daughter spent time in a climate where they were encouraged to be tolerant of other people's beliefs, where people were respectful of authority, where language wasn't loose, where people had a sense of balance and rest, where parents were honored, where people were considerate of others, and where there was respect for possessions. I've been on teams where you had to lock up your possessions during games and practices or else you risked them being stolen. It compromises the fabric of a team's culture very quickly when you know someone is stealing in your own locker room. Nobody wants to be part of a culture where lying is allowed, and therefore tacitly encouraged.

Any team, club, organization, etc., whether spiritual or secular, is going to have some form of leadership. Respect for leadership is a foundational teaching in nearly every applicable setting, so why would any parent object to their child participating on a team where they are encouraged to respect their coach? They wouldn't. The values espoused in the first commandment are held almost universally, yet the inclusion of the word "commandment" suddenly makes it inappropriate for public schools. This is how intentional word choice can make all the difference.

Similarly, I can't imagine a parent would want a climate where a coach could swear and be mean-spirited toward their child without consequence. Or where people are such workaholics and so consumptive that they have broken relationships. Or where peers don't even care to be nice to one another. When you play out the opposite of the Ten Commandments, that's hell. The vast majority of people want their sons and daughters in communities where there's some measure of care and order, and respect for authority figures, possessions, and relationships.

Thus, if you covertly use the Ten Commandments to establish the culture of your program, people aren't going to push back. You don't have to say they're the Ten Commandments. You don't have to quote the values as Bible verses. You can just talk about the importance of principles and values to maintaining order and harmony within a team.

Even in programs where the emphasis is on winning, there's still a need for order. If all you want to do is accumulate wins, having a team where the coach isn't abusive and the players are receptive is considered helpful. When you're in an environment that is about winning above all, I think it's still in line with the philosophy to spell out the process for getting there. I would contend that happy players play better than unhappy players. I would contend that people, regardless of their spirituality, enjoy participating more when the people they are with care about them. In all these cases, if you have some discernment and creativity, you can marry a biblical philosophy with a secular setting without using any Bible verses or overtly Christian terms.

His Plan, Not Ours

When you share your philosophy about how you're going to treat your players with a prospective program, they may not hire you because of what you say about how you treat winning or the scoreboard. But the fascinating thing is, if you *do* win, organizations are going to tolerate a little bit of philosophy they don't understand because they see that what you're doing has an outcome that they want, fundamentally. The bottom line is "the heart of the king is in the hands of the Lord" (see Proverbs 21:1), and if He wants you to be somewhere, you're going to be there.

Even though Daniel was second in command in a foreign, foul, idolatrous country, he was put in a position of favor. Moses was exalted to a position where he was taking on Pharaoh—the most powerful man in the land, brought to his knees by God, through Moses. We realize that nothing can stop a plan when it is His will. So, have a conviction, come up with a good plan, then execute the plan. See if the Lord won't want to raise you up into a position of impact outside of what would be expected.

No matter the setting, biblical principles are the best ways to treat people. Consider others better than yourself. Humility is going to be respected in places even if they don't care about God. In most places, they'll want some level of integrity, responsibility, and relational ability. Don't fear that you'll miss something. If God wants you there, you're going to be there. And if He doesn't, you won't; it doesn't matter how competent you are.

Reshaping a Culture

One of the most difficult things to do is to come into a Christian setting and try to implement To-By-For when the previous philosophy was Christian in name only, one that didn't share this philosophy's stance toward winning or how we treat opponents. That's the hardest fix. When a climate is biblical on its face but idolatrous when you open it up, the road to recovery is arduous.

I have been to Christian schools around the country and have seen an acknowledgement of Jesus in chapel services and posters in the hallway. However, when the heat is turned on in the gym or on the field of competition, I have seen many of those schools lose their testimony. I have seen Christian coaches and parents berate officials as calls went against their team. I attended one particular game between two Christian high schools where the officials were mistreated, and the parents were yelling at each other in the stands. It was an embarrassing moment for both schools that claimed to represent Christ. There didn't appear to be any vision for displaying the Kingdom of God, even in the midst of adversity, with bad calls supposedly going against their team and the outcome not going the way they had hoped.

On the other hand, secular climates often see our philosophy as a breath of fresh air. A coach who emphasizes treating both teammates and opponents with grace is a rare thing among secular programs. The resistance to To-By-For often seen in Christian programs can be shocking to experience if you haven't done it before or been given prior warning. While that may feel discouraging, I see it as just one more reason the mission field is the place to be. People in secular programs haven't been numbed to religion by complacent, lip-service Christianity.

What does it take to turn around a program? There are obviously adjustments that will be made. But as Dr. Coleman says in *Master Plan of Evangelism*, there are principles that are applicable at all levels of society, any year, any culture, any language—sports ministry included. Sports principles are business principles. They're principles that also offer wisdom for how to turn a family around, a business around, a school around, a team around.

Whatever the principles you incorporate into your culture are, prayer has to be a component of the final plan. The battle is not against flesh and blood. We cannot lose sight of the fact that this is a spiritual philosophy. If you don't see the enemy as an invisible being, then you're going to be compromised in terms of traction and opportunity. The invisible world is addressed through the Word of God and prayer and the visible world is addressed through words and action. This may sound obvious, but you would be surprised at how many people don't address the spiritual world at all when attempting to advance the Kingdom. But when you have a philosophy that's meant to evangelize and disciple at its core, you must have intentional, strategic prayer in your toolbox, or you'll never realize your goals.

Now that doesn't mean you won't win. It doesn't mean you won't play your sport well. That's an entirely different conversation. As we've said before, if you win championships but never strive to spread His Word, that would be a loss. Our primary target is eternity and the glory of God. The other targets are ancillary byproducts. You can also have these other things that are part of the trip, that can add to the enjoyment on this planet, but compared to eternity, they don't matter at all.

Visual Reminders

The power of words is significant, and words play an important role in how we can reshape a culture to be To-By-For. One way to effectively harness the power of words is with "plaques," or just any written statements that are visible—something that causes people to see a physical reminder of where we're going—the what, why, and how, written out for all to see.

God made humans. He knows how they're wired. They're driven significantly by what they hear and what they see. So, we leverage the principles of the Scriptures to advance the Kingdom. In terms of the sports climate, we use words that are spoken continuously and seen continuously as a stimulant to stay on a track toward the target. There's a reason to keep things in front of your face. Deuteronomy 6 advocates for speaking about things "when you lie down, when you get up, and when you walk along the road." It says to put your principles on the backs of your hands and on your doors and on your gates—visible truths that you both see and hear. Having these truths continuously prevalent increases the chances you'll stay on the narrow road.

In this philosophy, we practice that. If you're in a Christian climate, you can hang up plaques, posters, sayings, etc., with Bible verses that speak life and truth, around the locker rooms, in the halls, and in classrooms. If you're in a secular climate, however, you have to paraphrase biblical truth and life truth. All aspects of the heart, soul, and mind are leveraged by continuous articulation, verbally and visually, off and on the field. Philosophical positions must be communicated by words and action. This is not behavior modification; it's heart transformation.

This is part of the operating system of the coach or leader. We post things publicly and visibly. We talk about them all the time. What is the heart we want to see displayed; what are the attitudes that need to be changed? Under the To-By-For philosophy, the program is going to change from the inside out. The field is often the last place where change is going to be seen. Praying drives the invisible world. Words change the mind, emotion, will, and body.

For all this to take place, there has to be a clear vision. You, as a leader, or whoever is in charge, need to have a clear vision. Where are you headed as a program? Assistants have to share that vision. You have to have a plan, make sure it's a good plan, and execute the plan. At any point of those three components, you can go sideways.

There also has to be a clear mission statement. Vision is what you see and can't touch. Goals and the mission are things you can touch today. Who are we? What do we want to become as a program? It is going to be educational mentally, emotionally, and—depending on the program—spiritually. For example, in one program, I saw the plaque, "In all things at all times to the glory of God." This was obviously in a Christian setting. You can, however, paraphrase that.

A Vision That Is Not Your Own

When we are in a position where we are not the one who creates the vision for the program, oftentimes we're under somebody whose vision may be different than our own. In these cases, our job is to help our leader implement their vision.

But if we disagree with our leader's vision; what side are we on? What do we do then? I've worked for coaches whose main goal was the scoreboard. Sure, they cared about players, but not really on the deepest level. When we find ourselves in this spot we need to ask: can I work here? Can I work for this boss? The bottom line, in terms of submission to authority, is that you should either work for them with your whole heart or get out. Do not grumble and complain, be divisive, or implement a program contrary to their vision. Don't do it for the sake of a job because you need an income. It's a disservice to God and your boss and that organization for you to be there merely because you need a paycheck. God can provide for you without you being a hypocrite and undermining somebody else's mission.

Decide what things you can allow to exist and what you can't. Some people feel like they can go to a school where you can't pray. Others can't teach at a school that mandates certain things or negates other things. Most Jesus people in athletics and education work at schools where they're not allowed to do certain biblical things, and they somehow have found a way to navigate that. Some people may say, "If I can't share the gospel, I'm not going to work here."

Most of the staff in a program are assistants, not head coaches, and have the responsibility to implement the vision of the one who is over them. If you want the blessing of God, bless your authority figures. If you are in charge, have a clear vision for yourself, the other leadership, and your staff. There must be clear principles. What are the principles that will impact conduct? Write them down. Review them continually. Make them visible. Everybody has to know it and has to be able to execute it without conscious thought. Chances are that something will inevitably go sideways and leadership needs to be prepared to give an orderly response to the unknowns they run into.

Lead with Conviction

If you're going to change a program, you'll need to have strong conviction. You must "set your face like flint" (Isaiah 50:7), and be prepared to stick with the plan even if things go sideways. If it's a good plan, and it's the plan God's given you, there can be no second-guessing.

When I was a coach, I felt the Holy Spirit say to me, "This is My team. It's not your team. You happen to be the head coach, but it's My team. Those are My kids. I want you to run it My way, not your way. I promise you I'm going to command you to do certain things that are unorthodox because I'm unorthodox and if you follow Me you're going to be unorthodox, because I want to see if you're willing to be a fool for Christ and it's going to risk your reputation and even compromise the scoreboard at times. But this is about Me and My glory and your submission and obedience to Me. So you do what I say, not what you think is right. I'm going to offend your mind, your emotions, and your will at times."

This is how the Kingdom works. He is non-traditional. And you'd better be willing to hit the curveball because He doesn't just throw it straight and make it simple. That's when you serve the Lord. Every step along the way needs to be taken in service of His Kingdom. You figure out your plan, make sure it's a good plan, articulate your principles, execute the plan, and have the conviction to stick it out when it doesn't work—all in His name.

If you want a program, and you want His will, He'll hear you and He'll give it to you. I can't tell you when or how. But He will be glorified because He will not be mocked. That doesn't mean it's going to work in the world's eyes. It doesn't mean it's going to work for you. He will receive glory for Himself. And you will be blessed.

Discussion Questions

1. *Implementing Biblical Principles in Secular Environments:* How can a coach or administrator balance the desire to incorporate biblical values into a secular sports program while being sensitive to the cultural and legal limitations they may face?

2. *The Role of Prayer in Secular Settings:* In secular environments where openly sharing the gospel may not be permitted, how can coaches and leaders use prayer strategically, both for themselves and their teams, without violating policies or alienating others?

3. *Influence of Words in Shaping Team Culture:* How can the strategic use of language and values (such as the Ten Commandments presented in a secular way) impact the culture of a sports team, and what challenges might arise when trying to implement this approach?

4. *Navigating Leadership with a Different Vision:* If you find yourself in a leadership position under a coach or authority with a different vision than your own, how can you respectfully support their vision while maintaining your own integrity and commitment to biblical values?

THE CHAMPION'S MANIFESTO

By Scotty Kessler

True CHAMPIONS are made, not born. CHAMPIONS are made in adversity. Bad days, problems, heartaches, and losses are all necessary elements in molding CHAMPIONS.

Character is built in the storm. It is not built in prosperity; it is built in adversity. You develop strength when you are in trouble. Learning to handle opposition rightly will make you a CHAMPION.

CHAMPIONS don't let their circumstances affect their character. Bad games, bad plays, bad breaks do not change their will to prepare, or their will to strive and fight for excellence every chance they get . . . every day . . . all day long.

CHAMPIONS will inspire their teammates to play harder, more intensely, by their example. They walk their talk.

CHAMPIONS are interested in learning all they can, mastering skills and responsibilities, and acquiring every characteristic that helps them gain the edge.

A CHAMPION is not an individual star necessarily, but a team player who knows how to function with others.

A CHAMPION lives above pressure but thrives on it.

A CHAMPION is willing to pay the price—whatever it takes!

A CHAMPION is single-minded in purpose.

A CHAMPION is not sidetracked by distractions or by things that do not help them reach their goals.

A CHAMPION knows that winning is a by-product of being committed to excellence; winning takes care of itself.

A CHAMPION lets nothing interfere with their priority: becoming the best they possibly can become.

CHAMPIONS hang around other CHAMPIONS because they want to be influenced by each other's character. Nothing hinders them from their goal.

CHAMPIONS love competition: the challenge of becoming more disciplined, more intense, more prepared. They realize the harder the battle is, the greater the adversity—the stronger they'll become and the quicker they'll achieve their goals.

CHAMPIONS relish the battle. They are driven to excel.

CHAMPIONS are never satisfied with their performance, but are always content with the fact that they are continually striving to get better.

CHAMPIONS are uncomfortable with imperfection—always pursuing perfection, while knowing it can never fully be reached, but loving the battle of trying to reach it. They fight for excellence!

CHAMPIONS are committed to excellence . . . always . . . only.

The difference between CHAMPIONS and everyone else is very simple: CHAMPIONS are always willing to do the "little things." That's the simple difference.

Being a CHAMPION has nothing to do with being #1, or the amount of playing time a person gets. In fact, being a CHAMPION is not exclusively a characteristic of athletes—there are CHAMPIONS in all facets of life: students can become CHAMPIONS, parents also . . . anyone can! We're talking about character, not winning and losing— CHAMPIONSHIP CHARACTER!

CHAMPIONS don't care whether there are five or 50,000 people at the game . . . or even if it's a game or practice. They only know that each and every situation is a chance, a chance to improve.

CHAMPIONS are not affected by scoreboards or team records. Whether the score is 50–0 or 0–50, whether their record is 0–10 or 10–0, they play the same and they practice the same: all out!

CHAMPIONS never worry about things they can't control, they realize they can only control themselves and their attitude.

CHAMPIONS never quit. They don't even know what the word "quit" means. They only know to keep working, to keep striving—regardless of circumstances.

CHAMPIONS know that to be a CHAMPION they must be committed to excellence in everything they do, in every situation, whether at home, at school, at work, or at play. They realize that it is impossible to be committed to excellence in one thing and not another, because being a CHAMPION is not what you do but who you are: it's character!

CHAMPIONS never make excuses, grumble, complain, point fingers, or talk about other people. They only talk about how they can get better.

CHAMPIONS thrill to the joy of the struggle!

CHAMPIONS know they have to learn to serve—before they will ever know how to lead.

CHAMPIONS never desire their opponents fail or get injured. In fact, they actually want them to play well, because the better the opposition plays, the greater the CHAMPION is challenged to perform! It is a double win!

The CHAMPION'S theme is "Competition Breeds Excellence."

The mark of a CHAMPION is hard work—they work when no one is watching.

CHAMPIONS realize that sometimes they fail, maybe often and over and over. But they know that what makes them a CHAMPION is how they respond each time they fail. Champions choose to forget their failures, and fight on again.

The mark of a CHAMPION is how they respond each time they fail.

The CHAMPION chooses to forget their failures and fight on again. Their motto is "knocked down seven times, get up eight!"

Being a CHAMPION has nothing to do with success and failure on the scoreboard; it has to do with choosing to have a CHAMPION-SHIP CHARACTER every moment of every day.

CHAMPIONS realize that some days, even most days, they don't "feel" like working, striving, or paying the price to become a CHAMPION. But then they remember, or another CHAMPION reminds them, that being a CHAMPION is a choice they make over and over and over each day, and so they make that choice again.

Above all, being—becoming—a CHAMPION is a choice you make each day.

What will you choose?

ATTRIBUTES OF A "SPECIAL" BASEBALL TEAM

You know you have a special baseball team when you see these things:

- When everyone shows up to meetings five minutes early
- When players who are going to be late or will not be able to show up for a baseball-related activity communicate in advance to inform and explain
- When no one "walks" on the playing field at any time during a practice session . . . they are always "on the hop"
- When after practice, reps, everyday drills, and swings in the cages, individuals give encouraging feedback—"put ups"—to a teammate
- When players learn how to stay as completely focused and intense for a to-to-three-hour practice as a game (for game-time intensity and concentration)
- When players who are frustrated with the play (or with a particular play} don't show it but simply "go back to work"
- When players move on and off the field in between innings with urgency
- When players are as excited about their teammates' success as they are about their own success
- When hitters love bunting, hit and run, and hitting behind runners just as much as "taking hacks"
- When players look the coach in the eye when he or she is giving them feedback and correction, and are humble and teachable in response

- When these things are done not because you "have to" but because you "want to"
- When players are out before practice begins, working on their skill drills and goal sets . . . always taking advantage of opportunities to improve
- When players stay out after practice officially ends to do extra conditioning or work on any areas of their play that need improvement
- When someone makes a special play on the field and eight other guys on the field and the entire dugout acknowledge it
- When the practice field is filled with guys who are smiling, whether they "feel like it" or not—simply loving the pleasure of playing the game of baseball and being together
- When upperclassmen see their role as being servant leaders to the underclassmen
- When upperclassmen pick up the field, locker room, bus, or dugout, whether they made the mess or not
- When players cover for each other when gear, clothing items, or equipment are left on the field, locker room, or bus
- When players treat their coaches, teammates, opponents, and umpires with respect, regardless of whether they think they deserve it or not
- When players greet each other with a kind word and/or handshake in the locker room, cafeteria, and hallways of the school
- When players sit up in their chairs during meetings and fill the front rows of the meeting room and classroom, and have their eyes focused on the coach when he speaks
- When every player is backing up every play on the field for any possible situation
- When players fully realize the universal truth that more games are lost than are won, making them more apt to take seriously the little things that enhance their opportunities for success each season

These "little things" are very difficult to do, because "doing the right thing" rarely comes naturally. I'm not saying that if you do not do these "little things" you will not succeed. I'm only saying that if you do not consider doing these things, then there is a very small chance the team will reach its fullest potential, for when you do the "little things," the "big things" take care of themselves.

IF SOMETHING IS IMPORTANT ENOUGH TO DO,
THEN IT IS IMPORTANT TO DO IT RIGHT.

ACKNOWLEDGMENTS

From Tim Kuykendall

I would like to acknowledge Scotty Kessler as the architect of the *Competing Biblically* philosophy. For those of you who know "Kess," you understand that he never wants any credit or acknowledgment. He truly lives out "for the glory of God" more than anyone I know.

There are countless lives that have been impacted by Scotty Kessler and this philosophy of competition. His impact goes beyond words on a page, or a philosophy, as he has lived out what it looks like to be a discipler, pray-er, and epitome of the To-By-For Great Commission lifestyle. I know I speak for many when I say I am grateful Scotty Kessler has been my mentor for many years. My life would have looked so much different if God had not put Kess in my life.

For this reason, I say a heartfelt "Attaway" to you, Kess.

I also want to thank my wife, Heather Buck Kuykendall, for the encouragement to finish this book, to help be a part of the legacy of *Competing Biblically* and finally get it in print. I love you, Heather!

I would also like to acknowledge Brian Peterson, my friend and fellow co-founder of Reality Sports, in Washington State. We were two young guys attempting to do sports ministry when we embraced the *Competing Biblically* philosophy and morphed it into our own "Competing Upside Down" message, with Kess cheering us on along the way.

Finally, I would like to thank Arlyn Lawrence, our editor from Inspira Literary Solutions. Her gifting, experience, and Spirit-led life have been instrumental of bringing together hundreds of pages and notebooks on this topic of faith and sport. Thanks also to editor Timothy Lawrence, for his insightful editing and input. Thank you, Team Inspira!

From Scotty Kessler

I would like to acknowledge the late Frosty Westering, my Head Football Coach at Pacific Lutheran University in Tacoma, Washington, and my primary mentor in all things related to integrating sport and faith. Without question, from start to finish, Frosty was the key and most prominent voice of instruction that unlocked my spirit, soul and body, in what it meant and means to compete biblically.

Also, many thanks to Wes Neal, who lit a fire in my soul 50 years ago in articulating how the Lord wishes to live and play through us, like a hand fits in a glove, through his benchmark book on the subject, *The Handbook on Athletic Perfection.*

I would also like to acknowledge the many coaching colleagues, teammates, and players who have been part of my personal story over the years, who inspired me and gave me glimpses of what it looks like to compete biblically.

Finally, and most importantly, I would like to thank my wife, Tammy, and my children, Taylor, Reid, and Rylee for giving me the freedom to partner around the country with others wishing to integrate sport and faith these last 19 years.

Thanks be to God for these indescribable gifts, in Jesus' name.

ABOUT THE AUTHORS

Tim Kuykendall has over 30 years of coaching experience. He was an All-Pac 10 outfielder and Pac 10 North MVP as a baseball player at Washington State University, and was selected as one of the Top 50 players in the Washington State University Baseball's History and inducted into the Butte College Athletics Hall of Fame in 2019 as a player. As a coach, he coached at his alma mater, WSU, and then began a successful, 23-year high school baseball coaching career in Washington State. He was honored in June of 2023 to be inducted into the Washington State Baseball Coaches Hall of Fame. In 2006, Tim co-founded Reality Sports, a sports ministry outside of Seattle, WA, where he served as the Director of Baseball. He also served as the chaplain for the Tacoma Rainiers, AAA affiliate of the Seattle Mariners, for 15 years. Currently, Tim and his wife Heather reside in Maui, Hawaii, where he serves as Director of Athletics for Vertical Sports Maui. Tim and Heather are the proud parents of three grown children, grandparents to one granddaughter, and devoted caretakers of two golden retrievers that are loved like family.

Scotty Kessler is the Director of The Robert Coleman School of Discipleship and The Wes Neal School of Sports Ministry at Faith International University and Seminary in Tacoma (Washington). His current focus is in international ministry, through which he regularly visits Jerusalem to pray for its peace and blessing. Additionally, he is a consultant on initiatives related to prayer, discipleship, and the integration of sport and faith. Scotty lives in Fort Myers, Florida with his wife Tammy and their daughter; they also have two grown sons.